OCT - 9 2015

SPIRITUAL
TELEPATHY

SPIRITUAL TELEPATHY

ANCIENT TECHNIQUES TO ACCESS THE WISDOM OF YOUR SOUL

COLLEEN MAURO

This publication has been generously supported by
The Kern Foundation

QUEST
BOOKS

Theosophical Publishing House
Wheaton, Illinois * Chennai, India

Quest Books
PO Box 270
Wheaton, IL 60187-0270

www.questbooks.net

Cover photo by Antonio M. Rosario
Cover design by Greta Polo
Typesetting by DataPage, Inc.

Library of Congress Cataloging-in-Publication Data

Mauro, Colleen.
    Spiritual telepathy: ancient techniques to access the wisdom of your soul / Colleen Mauro.—First Quest Edition.
        pages   cm
    Includes bibliographical references and index.
        ISBN 978-0-8356-0931-9
    1. Spiritual life.   2. Spirituality.   3. Occultism.   4. Religion.
    5. Telepathy.   I. Title.
    BF1999.M445 2015
    204—dc23   2014036820

5   4   3   2   1   *   15   16   17   18   19   20

Printed in the United States of America

For my beloved Ken

*And he dreamed, and behold, a ladder set up
on the earth, and the top of it reached to heaven.*

—Genesis 28:12

CONTENTS

Acknowledgments

My deepest thanks to:

The staff at Quest Books: editors Richard Smoley, Sharron Dorr, and Martha Woolverton; publicity director Jessica Salasek; and production manager Nancy Grace.

My dear friend and colleague Hal Zina Bennett, who helped in so many ways right from the start—from referrals to the freelance editing jobs that kept me afloat while I worked on the manuscript, to expert advice on the book proposal, to the lively e-mail correspondence that made my solitary days more interesting and enjoyable.

LaUna Huffines, Steven Lumiere, Corinne McLaughlin, Steve Nation, Jan Skogstrom, Nancy Seifer, Barbara Valocore, and Martin Vieweg, who all graciously agreed to share their experiences with the Wisdom teachings; Greg Bogart, Lorre Eaton, Matthew Gilbert, Ray Grasse, Steven Lumiere, Corinne McLaughlin, Laurel Mellin, Steve Nation, and Martin Vieweg, who read all or parts of the manuscript and provided helpful feedback; Jennifer Anderson, Bobbi Ingram, Barbara Morgan, Sandra Mussey, Debara Zahn, and my sister Lori Cooper, who provided ongoing support and encouragement.

Eric Heideman, my "personal librarian" who took an interest in my project and cheerfully tracked down many hard to find books for me.

Lucis Trust, for my Arcane School training and for allowing me to adapt—and in many places reinterpret—their meditations, seed thoughts, and prayers/affirmations for this book.

Finally, the two people I would most like to thank are Jean Kellett, who introduced me to the subject of spiritual telepathy and inspired my exploration of this topic; and, especially, my long-time partner Kenneth Bowser. His love and support made this book possible.

INTRODUCTION

This is a book about the hidden potential of the human mind. In this book, I will introduce you to ancient mind-training techniques that will allow you to access the wisdom and guidance of your own soul.

These techniques come from a body of knowledge called the Ageless Wisdom. These teachings, also known as the esoteric—or mystery—teachings, have been described as "mankind's most sacred treasure . . . the knowledge which will allow us to access the powers that [lie] dormant in the human mind."[1] Once taught in the ancient mystery schools of Egypt, Greece, Babylon, and India, these teachings were first put into book form by the Hindu sage Patanjali, author of *The Yoga Sutras*.

In this classic book, Patanjali taught a system of mind control called raja yoga, which focused on the higher potential of the mind. Patanjali taught that the mind has two levels—the lower or rational mind and the higher or intuitive mind. The soul, our gateway to the higher worlds, is the link between our higher and lower minds. When we train the lower mind to make contact with the soul, the soul transmits information from the higher mind to our brains. We then have direct access to the subtle worlds where information on all subjects can be found.

When we build our bridge between the lower mind and the soul, we become pioneers in the next stage of human development—the soul-aligned human being. The soul-aligned human has a mind trained to "see" in two directions: outward into the physical world or upward into the subtle worlds of spirit. A new level of awareness becomes possible as our focus shifts from the physical to the subtle planes. We find our place within the greater whole and experience the oneness of all life. We move from the personal to the universal, from "me" to "we."

The catastrophic problems we face today are speeding up the usual slow pace of evolution and calling forth this expansion in human consciousness. With our social and ecological systems in crisis, our very survival is dependent on our ability to shift from self-interest to serving the greater good of the entire human family.

When we build our bridge to the soul, we become part of a growing army of "practical" mystics; our feet are on the ground, but our minds are trained to access the subtle realms, where higher levels of wisdom and knowledge can be found. At this time of upheaval and change, we need access to these higher sources of wisdom and guidance as never before. As Albert Einstein famously said, the problems in our world cannot be solved by the same level of thinking that created them. The catastrophic problems we face today require a higher level of wisdom and insight.

When we make contact with the soul, our life purpose, our service to humanity, becomes clear. Each of us has a task, a contribution to make to the world, and, at this critical period, we are all urgently needed. As I will show you in this book, our most celebrated creative thinkers—those people we call geniuses or visionaries—have all had the ability to access the higher worlds. But it's not just the famous; I will also introduce you to "ordinary" people who have gained access to that universal wellspring of creativity and inspiration—people who are living a life of spiritual purpose and service.

Since the information we receive from the subtle worlds, on all levels, is always telepathic, this experience is called *spiritual telepathy*. It was an experience of spiritual telepathy that led to the launch of *Intuition* magazine in the late 1980s. In 1988, after working in alternative magazine publishing for several years, I was between jobs and pondering my next move. I was living in San Francisco, which at that time was not known as a place to pursue a career in magazine publishing. Since most of the publishing jobs were in Los Angeles, New York, or Boston, I was lucky to have found three back-to-back jobs in the Bay Area. But now, with no job offers in sight, my luck seemed to be running out.

My days were spent researching new magazines, sending out resumes, and worrying about my rapidly diminishing bank account. I was also worried that I might have to leave San Francisco, a city I loved. One morning, I decided to treat myself to a worry-free day outdoors, working in my backyard garden. I enjoyed the sunny October day as I weeded the flower beds, planted tulip bulbs, and raked leaves. I was standing with the rake in my hand when a thought suddenly flashed through my mind: *The Center for Applied Intuition*. This wasn't the familiar type of intuitive experience—the subtle emotional or body-based sensation of knowing—but a purely mental experience. The name had simply appeared, fully formed, as though someone had dropped the words directly into my brain. I immediately knew it wasn't my thought, and it certainly made no logical sense. I knew about the center and had met its founder, a former scientist from the Stanford Research Institute named Bill Kautz. I knew the center sponsored intuition development trainings and conferences; I also knew they had a team of expert intuitives who provided consultations to individuals and business owners. Since I knew Bill had a two-room office and a very small staff, I didn't see the point of contacting him. I was looking for a magazine job, not an administrative position.

I mulled it over for a few days and then called Bill to ask for information about the center's activities. A few days later a large manila envelope arrived. Inside, I found several brochures and a simple, typewritten journal called *Applied Psi*, the quarterly publication Bill sent to the center's two hundred members. The journal, devoted to the development of intuition and creativity, was fascinating. As I flipped through the pages, I suddenly had an idea: with a different format and a new name, this could be a real magazine, one that would appeal to an audience far beyond the center's small membership.

I called Bill and made an appointment to speak with him the following week. The more I thought about it, the more sense it made. I had long studied the intuitive arts, and this project would be the perfect marriage of my interests and experience.

When I arrived at the center, I explained my idea to Bill. He immediately lit up and told me he had always dreamed of turning *Applied Psi* into a real magazine, but the right person had never come along. I went home and banged out a proposal, came back the next day, and *Intuition: A Magazine for the Higher Potential of the Mind* was born.

From the start, it was my baby. Since the center had such limited space, I set up shop at my dining room table. I cajoled writer friends into contributing free articles, sold advertising space to pay for the printing, and set up local bookstore distribution. When all the copies sold out, I knew my hunch had been right. I set up a national newsstand distribution network and started work on the second issue. When Bill decided to close the center, he signed the rights to *Intuition* over to me. I later received a grant to set up an office and hire a staff. During the seven years I published the magazine, the circulation steadily grew, eventually reaching a readership of over sixty thousand.

When I started the magazine, there were only two popular books on the subject: Frances Vaughan's *Awakening Intuition* and Philip Goldberg's *The Intuitive Edge*. In the years since, there has been a seemingly endless stream of books published on this topic. Intuition, it seems, is now a household word. No longer just the province of women and creative artists, intuition is now a part of daily life for a wide range of people—from businesspeople to politicians to police detectives. Now that the practice of intuition is an accepted part of our culture, it's time to take the next step and explore a more advanced form of spiritual perception.

It is now commonly accepted that we have ways of knowing and accessing information beyond the range of our five senses. These senses—hearing, touch, taste, sight, and smell—have allowed us to experience the physical plane. But, as the Wisdom teachings tell us, we have other planes to discover and more subtle senses to unfold. These teachings tell us that our true sixth sense is the mind. Once trained, the mind becomes our "telescope," the tool we use to peer into the subtle worlds.

Our personal intuition provides us with guidance about our work, our relationships, and other aspects of our day-to-day lives. When we build our bridge to the soul, we have the ability to register thoughts and ideas from a much higher source—the universal, or divine, mind—the storehouse of all wisdom and knowledge.

I didn't have a name for my intuitive experience until I was introduced to the subject by a friend and colleague many years later. Soon afterward, I began to study the Wisdom literature, reading my way through the works of Alice Bailey and many other authors. Although the Bailey books had been highly recommended, I had resisted reading them for years. Always on the go, I was intimidated by their density and length and felt more than a little skeptical about this kind of material.

In these books I found a Wisdom teaching that dates back to the earliest days of humanity—a universal doctrine that forms the core of all our great religions. These teachings have appeared in different forms in various places throughout history, each in a form suitable to its time and place. In the West, these teachings were passed along by a "golden chain" of adepts that included Pythagoras and Plato.[2] What had once been a secret teaching given only to initiates was first presented to the public in a series of books in the nineteenth and twentieth centuries. These books—*The Secret Doctrine* by Helena Blavatsky, founder of the Theosophical Society, and the book series by Alice Bailey and Helena Roerich—educated a new generation of spiritual seekers.

I was particularly intrigued by the information on spiritual telepathy. I have always felt deeply touched—and envious—when reading of those able to communicate with the spiritual world. I loved the story of Joan of Arc and the divine voices that urged her to save France from English domination during the Hundred Years War. I loved reading about Eileen Caddy and the divine guidance that led to the founding of the Findhorn community; I also enjoyed reading about the botanist George Washington Carver, who walked in the woods each morning to talk to God. I've always wondered, is it only special people—people more evolved than I am—who can have these experiences? Are they somehow preordained? Do we have to enter a monastery like the early Christian mystics did and devote our entire lives to spiritual practice?

As I studied this topic, it became clear that not only are such experiences possible for every one of us, they are our evolutionary destiny. Many spiritual leaders, philosophers, and scientists tell us that we are poised on the brink of an evolutionary leap, one as profound as our emergence from animal to human. When we link the lower mind with the soul, we take our first steps into the subtle worlds and cross the boundary from human to superhuman development.

The need to harness the untapped power of the mind is the underlying theme in Dan Brown's novel *The Lost Symbol.* In this book, Brown tells us that "mankind's disparate philosophies have all concurred on one thing . . . that a great enlightenment is coming . . . and the result will be the transformation of our human minds into their true potentiality."[3]

The Ageless Wisdom teachings have long provided the disciplines necessary to move us along this evolutionary path. These teachings add the mind to the heart-centered way of the mystic. According to Bailey, esotericism is a science: "the science of the soul—with its own terminology, experiments, deductions and laws."[4] The "high prize" of esoteric work is to become sensitive to the subtle worlds, to tap in to universal truths and knowledge and to bring down these divine ideas to help others—and the world.

At an earlier point in our history, knowledge of the outer world was paramount to our survival. In the past four centuries, our focus has been on the development of the rational mind. Our educational system has made it possible to develop our rational minds to the very peak of their power. But as many spiritual leaders tell us, our next evolutionary frontier is the conscious use of an even higher mental faculty—a purely intuitive means of accessing information. We are hovering on the borders of new knowledge, and it is our privilege to be the pioneers.

In my adult life, I have seen the step-by-step evolution of this field. In the 1970s, our focus was on psychic development, and a flood of psychic development courses, books, and schools appeared. Many of us had our favorite psychics on speed dial, asking for information and guidance on subjects both cosmic and mundane. Channeling became popular in the '80s. We were still relying on outside sources for wisdom and guidance, but now the information came from discarnate entities both great and small. By the '90s, the focus had shifted to intuition as we learned to access our own innate, inner wisdom.

By the turn of the century, there was an explosion of interest in the "extended," or "nonlocal," mind. After the release of the classified documents on Project Stargate—the secret, CIA-funded "remote viewing" experiments—a flood of books, articles, and trainings appeared on this topic. The work of pioneering scientists such as Dean Radin, Rupert Sheldrake, and Russell Targ has shown us that the mind is not confined within the brain. Their many experiments have provided evidence that the nonlocal mind can reach beyond the brain to gather information and affect people at a distance.

As the Wisdom teachings tell us, the mind has an even higher function: it can also be trained to extend "vertically" to register and record the wisdom found in the higher planes. When we link our higher and lower minds, traditional forms of channeling and mediumship become obsolete. Once trained, the mind becomes our own internal search engine; it extends out into the cosmos, gathers information, and then "downloads" that information directly into our brains.

To illustrate the universal nature of these teachings, I've included information on a wide range of cultures and spiritual traditions, both ancient and modern. I will also show you the ways in which science is now validating this ancient wisdom. It has been said that only when science and mysticism meet will we have a true picture of reality. The recent discoveries in quantum science have moved these two worlds closer than ever before. Quantum scientists have discovered that a sea of interactive, interconnected energy underlies the physical world. They have also provided us with evidence that suggests that we, too, are part of this energetic field. What they haven't—and *can't*—tell us is exactly *how* this occurs. The answer, according to the Wisdom teachings, is to be found in the subtle, not the physical, worlds. Science can measure and map the physical world, but until we have more sensitive scientific instruments, we can only explore the subtle worlds with our own inner "instrument"—the trained mind.

The former astronaut Edgar Mitchell is one scientist who believes that inner exploration is necessary to give us a complete picture of our world. In his book *The Way of the Explorer: An Apollo Astronaut's Journey through the Material and Mystical Worlds*, he writes:

> As I studied the beliefs of mystics . . . it became absolutely clear to me that first-person experiences, the subjective, with all its potential for misinterpretation, was just as important to understanding reality as the third-person observations of science. Nature has provided a broader range of mental capabilities than can be captured within the norms of Western cultural tradition."[5]

To bridge the gap between the physical and subtle worlds, we need more "inner scientists" trained to explore and chart this territory. In the past, we've had only the testimony of "special" people—the saints, mystics, and founders of our great spiritual traditions—to tell us about the subtle worlds. The tide of evolution has brought us to the point where many of us can open to the subtle worlds—without spending years in a monastery. It takes only the willingness to commit to a daily spiritual practice.

Most of the books on this topic are written in dense and arcane language. My goal is to make these teachings accessible to a wider audience and to provide you with a step-by-step method for linking your lower mind with the soul. During the ten years that I studied this subject, I read widely, became a student in the Arcane School, a multiyear esoteric training program, and interviewed many practitioners of the Wisdom tradition. I will share my personal experiences as I explored these teachings and introduce you to others who have also used these practices.

These practices have had a profound effect on my life. I have a deeper connection to my soul, a more consistent source of guidance, and a greater understanding of the contribution I can make to the world. The experience that led to the launch of *Intuition* magazine was spontaneous, but it is possible for each of us to build our bridge to the soul and register information from the higher worlds at will.

The meditations you'll find here are the most important part of this book. A regular meditation practice is essential for anyone who wants to access the higher worlds. It is only after we learn to quiet our minds and emotions that the brain can register the wisdom of the soul. This is a subtle process that comes about over time, through consistent daily practice.

In the first three chapters, I will take you on a Magical Mystery Tour as I explain the key principles of the Wisdom teachings. These chapters provide a foundation for the practices you'll find in this book. These chapters will give you an overview of our subtle anatomy and describe the ways we both send and receive telepathic information. I will also describe the differences between the three aspects of the mind and show you how this teaching appears in other spiritual traditions.

In chapter 4, I describe the three types of telepathy: instinctive, mental, and spiritual. In chapter 5, you will learn how to prepare your physical, emotional, and mental bodies for the influx of higher energies. In the remaining chapters, you will learn how to build your bridge to the subtle worlds and access the wisdom of your soul. I've also provided meditations that will help you to understand your higher purpose and individual avenue of service.

Those of you who build this bridge are the pioneers who will lead the way to a new civilization. And each of you who takes this step will make it easier for those who follow. When we build our bridge between the physical and spiritual worlds, we are, literally, bringing heaven down to earth. As more and more of us open to the subtle worlds, we will bring an ever-increasing flow of divine ideas and inspiration to the world. Together, we can usher in a new era of unity, cooperation, and peace.

One final note: As you read through this book, you will see the unavoidable use of the word *man*. In this context, remember that *man* refers, not to sexual gender, but to the original Sanskrit definition of the word as "the one who thinks."

Chapter One

THE EVOLUTIONARY JOURNEY

If men and women have come up from the beasts,
then they will likely end up with the gods.

—Ken Wilber

As I mentioned in the introduction, many spiritual leaders, philosophers, and scientists tell us that we stand at the threshold of an evolutionary shift, one as profound as our emergence from animal to human. Our next evolutionary breakthrough is not a change in form, but the emergence of a new type of human, the soul-aligned human being. When we align the lower self, or personality, with the higher self, or soul, an evolutionary step is taken. We take our first steps out of the human kingdom and into the superhuman worlds.

According to the Ageless Wisdom teachings, this development is part of a planned evolutionary sequence, our slow, step-by-step journey from human to divine. This journey takes us from the primitive life of the caveman to the superhuman state symbolized by the Christ, the Buddha, and other great spiritual leaders. This journey is illustrated by two biblical stories: the story of Adam and Eve in the Old Testament and the New Testament story of the Prodigal Son. The unfolding miracle begins when the divine spark in each of us descends into the physical world. This descent of spirit into matter is called the "involutionary" journey, or in the Hindu texts, the *pravritti marga*, the "path of outgoing."

In the Old Testament story, Adam and Eve are cast out of the Garden of Eden, a state of communion and bliss, into the physical world of space and time. This journey creates our illusion of separateness as we lose our conscious connection to the Divine. Once on earth, through a long cycle of rebirth, we undergo a process of gradual awakening. It is then that our evolutionary journey, our climb from dust to the stars, begins.

The evolutionary journey, the path of return, is illustrated by the New Testament story of the Prodigal Son. In this tale, the son leaves his father's house for a journey to "the far country." He squanders his inheritance on wild living and soon finds himself broke and alone. Eventually, after much suffering, he "comes to himself" and makes the decision to "arise and go" back to his father's house—a concise description of the classic spiritual journey.

We are living in a time of accelerated opening, and it is now possible to take the next step up the evolutionary ladder. As I've mentioned, the higher self, or soul, our spark of the Divine, is our portal to the superhuman worlds. The soul is neither spirit nor matter but our link between the two. The soul stands midway between the personality and the world of pure spirit.

When we build our bridge to the soul, we enlarge our horizons and expand our consciousness beyond the boundaries of the physical world. We become aware of a new kingdom in nature: the fifth kingdom, the kingdom of the soul. When we gain access to this higher realm, a new world opens before us. Our history books are full of stories about our most famous explorers—from Christopher Columbus's journey to the Americas, to Neil Armstrong's walk on the moon. The next frontier is our exploration of the subtle world, a world once accessible only to mystics, seers, and spiritual leaders.

In the next three chapters, as I cover the key principles of the Wisdom tradition, I will describe the steps on this journey. I will introduce you to the worlds beyond the physical realm and describe our subtle anatomy—what the Wisdom teachings call the "spiritual constitution of man." This will give you the necessary framework to understand the teachings and practices presented in this book.

You'll see how, as we move up the evolutionary ladder, our perceptual abilities evolve from the instinct of the animal to the intellect of modern man, to the pure intuitive knowing of the soul-aligned human being. You'll see how each aspect of this teaching fits together like a piece of a larger puzzle—a wisdom "that God hid in a mystery"; one that "an eye has not seen, an ear has not heard and no human mind has conceived"; a wisdom that "God destined for our glory before time began" (1 Cor. 2:9). We begin with a look at the sacred number seven.

THE SACRED NUMBER SEVEN

Pythagoras, said to be the world's first philosopher, was born in Greece in the sixth century BCE. After studying in the mystery schools of Egypt and Babylon, he settled in Croton, in Southern Italy, where he created a mystery school of his own. Pythagoras, who believed geometry to be one of the three sciences essential to the understanding of God, taught spiritual principles through the study of numbers. For Pythagoras, Number was "the principle of rational order in the universe, the source and the root of all things, both universal and divine." According to Pythagoras, seven is the number of religion and spiritual law, as man is controlled by "the seven celestial spirits," the biblical "Seven Spirits before the Throne."[1]

Pick up any book on the Wisdom tradition and you're sure to come across the number seven. In the Wisdom teachings there are seven planes of consciousness; seven kingdoms in nature; seven senses; seven sacraments; seven initiations; seven energy centers, or chakras; and seven "races," or stages of human development. This number is also repeated in the material world, where we have seven continents, seven seas, seven days of the week, seven elements, seven notes in an octave, seven major glands in the human body—even seven colors in a rainbow.

Like so many others, I was curious about the significance of this number and finally found an explanation in Helena Blavatsky's *The Secret Doctrine*. As Blavatsky points out, the square has long been the symbol of the material world. It symbolizes the four directions (east, west, north, and south) and the four races of man (black, white, red, and yellow). The three-sided triangle is symbolic of the trinity—a concept found in every religion—and of the spiritual world. Spirit combined with matter equals consciousness or life. When the triangle is merged with the square, a seven-pointed star is created, symbolizing the alignment of heaven and earth. Blavatsky writes that "the number seven is the perfect and sacred number of this solar system. Everything in the metaphysical and physical universe is septenary." She also writes that we are "seven-fold beings," the universe in miniature, "the septenary microcosm, to the septenary macrocosm."[2] The seven planes are key to understanding our seven-fold nature.

THE SEVEN PLANES

According to the Ageless Wisdom, our universe consists of seven planes, or frequencies, often referred to as planes of consciousness.

These planes correspond to seven levels of spiritual awareness. Each plane represents a more advanced state of consciousness.

The seven planes include the physical, emotional, mental, buddhic, spiritual, monadic, and divine planes. Usually depicted with seven horizontal lines superimposed one above the other, these planes interpenetrate. Each plane is divided into seven subplanes, which correspond to the higher sevenfold division.

Also called *chambers*, *palaces*, *gates*, or *heavens*, these planes are gradations of energy from pure spirit to dense matter. The three top planes are the formless worlds of spirit. The three lowest planes are the three worlds of the human being. The fourth, or buddhic, plane is the plane where spirit and matter meet. Our evolutionary journey extends to the first five planes: the three human planes and the two superhuman planes above.

This teaching may seem esoteric, but, as you will see below, it can be found in all our spiritual traditions.

Hinduism teaches that there are seven stages or states of consciousness on the path to illumination. In Patanjali's *Yoga Sutras*, mention is made of the seven worlds that correspond to the seven states of being. The Hindu texts also include mention of the fourteen *lokas*, the Sanskrit word for "spheres" or "planes." The seven superior lokas are the seven "heavens," and the seven inferior lokas are the seven hells.[3]

This concept of seven heavens is also found in Islam, Judaism, Taoism, and Shamanism. According to Islamic tradition, the Prophet Mohammed made contact with Allah only after his journey through the seven heavens. During their pilgrimage to Mecca, Muslims honor this event by circling the Kaaba, Islam's holiest building, seven times. The *merkavah*, the earliest Jewish mystics, used meditation practices to ascend through seven heavens, or "palaces," in their attempt to experience "the glory of the Lord."[4]

For the early Taoists, the seven heavens were symbolized by the seven stars of the Big Dipper. In a meditation ritual they called "pacing the Dipper," they imagined these stars as a ladder to the seventh heaven—what they called "the garden of the immortals."[5] The Siberian shamans used a birch tree with seven notches or branches to represent the seven heavens. This tree, used in their initiation ceremonies, symbolized their journey to the higher realms.[6]

Initiation into the mysteries of Mithras, a Persian pre-Christian religious cult, involved seven stages that represented the soul's journey through the seven "gates of heaven."[7] The soul's journey through seven gates is also described in an ancient Egyptian funereal text called the Book of Gates.

In the Cherokee tradition, the seven states of consciousness are represented by the seven spokes on their medicine wheel. Each spoke represents one of seven paths of spiritual initiation: the North, South, East, and West paths, the above and below paths, and the final "within" path.[8]

In the book of Revelation, Jesus stands with seven stars in his right hand, and the number seven is woven throughout this symbolic book. As I'll show you in the next chapter, the seven seals, seven candlesticks, and seven churches all represent the seven stages of spiritual awakening.[9]

THE PHYSICAL PLANE

Our five senses have equipped us to function on the physical plane. As we move up the evolutionary ladder, we develop the subtle senses we need to experience the higher worlds.

The first plane is home to both our physical and etheric bodies. Our physical bodies are composed of the substances found on the lower three subplanes—solid, liquid, and gaseous. These substances, perceptible to our five senses, make up our bones, blood system, nervous system, brain, and endocrine glands. Symbolized by the earth element, this three-dimensional world is called *Bhu* in the Hindu tradition, *Assiyah* in the kabbalah, and the "world of nature and the body" by the Sufis.

Our etheric bodies are composed of the finer matter of the top four subplanes. The etheric or energy body, perceptible only to our subtle senses, is made up of a network of fine energy currents. Called the "golden bowl" in the Bible, this energy body extends beyond and interpenetrates our physical form.[10] These energy currents, emanating from one or more of the seven planes, circulate through and energize our physical bodies. When these lines of energy intersect, an energy center, or chakra, is formed.

Everything that exists in our solar system has an etheric form, and it is through our etheric bodies that we are connected to the web of all life. Our etheric bodies form part of the "universal ether" that connects everything in our world—rocks, plants, animals, planets, and stars. Our etheric bodies link the physical body with the subtle bodies described below. It is also the means by which we receive and transmit telepathic information. It is easy to understand how we can be affected by thought currents, distant healing—even the movement of the planets above us—when we realize we are connected through this energetic web to everyone and everything on our planet and beyond.

Our etheric bodies are also a part of the etheric body of the planet itself. As Chief Seattle, chief of the Suquamish Indians, wrote in his famous letter to the American Government in the 1800s, "All things are connected like the blood which unites one family. Whatever befalls the earth befalls the sons of the earth. Man did not weave the web of life, he is merely a strand of it. Whatever he does to the web, he does to himself."[11]

The experience of unity—when we suddenly have "eyes to see" this finer grade of matter—has been reported by mystics from the beginning of time. Astronaut Edgar Mitchell had this experience when he gazed at the earth from the window of the *Kittyhawk* as he and his fellow astronauts returned from the Apollo 14 lunar mission:

> As I looked at the earth . . . I felt an extraordinary personal connectedness with it. I experienced what has been described as an ecstasy of unity. I not only saw the connectedness, I felt it and experienced it sentiently. I was overwhelmed with the sensation of physically and mentally extending out in the cosmos. The restraints and boundaries of flesh and bone fell away.[12]

Mario Beauregard, author of *The Spiritual Brain,* had a similar experience while lying in bed during a bout with chronic fatigue syndrome. As Beauregard relates,

> The experience began with a sensation of heat and a tingling in the spine and chest areas. Suddenly, I merged with the infinitely loving Cosmic Intelligence and became united with everything in the cosmos. This unitary state of being . . . was timeless and accompanied by intense bliss and ecstasy. In this state, I experienced the basic interconnectedness of all things in the cosmos, this infinite ocean of life.[13]

In *A Mythic Life,* Jean Houston describes the sense of interconnection she experienced while staring out the window as a child:

> Everything around me, including myself, suddenly became part of a single Unity, a glorious symphonic resonance in which every part of the universe was a part of and illuminated every other part, and I knew that in some way it all worked together . . . the utter interpenetration and union of everything with the All That Is.[14]

As Above, so Below

As the early pioneers of quantum science discovered, the interconnection that exists in the subtle world is duplicated in the physical world. When these scientists investigated matter at the subatomic level, they made a surprising discovery. They discovered that matter, at its most fundamental level, is not solid or separate; it is instead a web of interconnected particles capable of exchanging information across space and time. They also discovered, as Lynne McTaggart recounts in *The Field*, that energy exists in the space between particles—what they call the "Zero Point Field." McTaggart points out that many of these pioneering scientists explored the Eastern spiritual traditions in an attempt to understand the deeper meaning of these startling new discoveries.[15] Erwin Schrödinger, one of the main contributors to quantum theory, studied the Vedas and other Hindu spiritual texts. According to Larry Dossey, Schrödinger, who believed science to be incapable of providing direct insight into the "nature of spirit," wrote of the need for a "blood transfusion" between Western science and the Eastern traditions. A true understanding of our interconnected universe, Schrödinger wrote, will come only when Eastern teachings are assimilated into Western science.[16]

The Astral/Emotional Plane

The sixth, or emotional, plane forms a bridge between the mind and the physical body. Our emotional bodies are made up of the matter of all its seven subplanes. This is the plane of emotion and desire. Here, physical sensation is transmuted into feeling. It is through our emotional bodies that we become sensitive to moods and feelings—both our own and those around us. Our emotional bodies permeate and surround our physical bodies. This is the luminous energy body, or "aura," seen by clairvoyants. Our emotional state creates the variety of colors seen by psychics—black for hatred and malice, red for anger, blue for spiritual devotion.

On this plane we find a more subtle version of our physical senses. Physical sight becomes *clairvoyance*, or "clear seeing," the abilty to see at a distance; hearing becomes *clairaudience*, or "clear hearing," the ability to hear beyond the range of normal perception; and touch becomes *psychometry*, the ability to receive psychic impressions by touching an object. Patanjali called these abilities the lower *siddhis*, or "psychic powers."

Due to the force of human emotion and desire, this dream-like realm, long symbolized by water, is called the plane of illusion. Here, psychic impressions are often distorted and unreliable. Strong, uncontrolled emotions—anger, resentment, hate, or jealousy—can create congestion in the emotional body. This congestion filters down to the physical body and can lead to a variety of diseases, including cancer and lung, liver, and heart problems.

Our emotional bodies can separate from the physical body while we sleep and move to distant locations with lightening speed, a phenomenon known as "astral travel." This four-dimensional world is called *Antariksa* in the Vedas, *Yetzirah* in the kabbalah, and the "realm of the senses" by the Sufis.

THE MENTAL PLANE

On the mental plane, sensation becomes perception. On this plane, we develop the powers of concrete thought, rationality, inspiration, and intuition. Here we are moved by ideas rather than emotions. On this plane, we rise above the murky depths of the emotional plane and see things clearly, free of the illusion and distortion of the astral realm.

The faculties of the lower mental body, made up of the substance of the four lower subplanes, are cognitive reasoning, thought, and memory. The higher mental world, called *arupa*, or "formless," is found on the top three subplanes. The faculties of the higher mental body include abstract reasoning, inspiration, and intuition. In his book on the mental body, A. E. Powell uses a mathematical analogy to describe the distinction between the lower and higher mental bodies. Basic arithmetic like adding, subtracting, and multiplying numbers belongs to the lower mental, while algebra—where symbols represent numbers—is analogous to the abstract level.[17]

The soul, called the "causal" body, is found on the third subplane. The causal body is, in the words of Saint Paul, "the house not made with hands, eternal in the heavens" (2 Cor. 5:1). The soul wisdom gained from the sum total of our many lifetimes is stored in this body.

As I mentioned above, our human personalities consist of our physical, emotional, and lower mental bodies. It is on the third subplane that the personality and soul meet. The link between the two is called the *Antahkarana*, or "Rainbow Bridge," a subject we will explore more fully in chapter 6. Saint Paul was speaking of this plane when he said, "I knew a man in Christ . . . caught up in the third heaven. . . . [He] was caught up into paradise" (2 Cor. 12:2).

The higher, or spiritual, mind is composed of the substance of only the last and highest mental subplane. When this level of consciousness is awakened, knowledge comes in the form of pure intuitive perception.

The Akashic Records, understood in esoteric thought as the complete history of each human being, can be found in this fifth-dimensional world.[18] Symbolized by fire, the mental plane is called

Mahendra in the Hindu scriptures, *Beriyah* in the kabbalah, and "the realm of the heart" by the Sufis.

The next two planes, the buddhic and spiritual planes, are the planes of spiritual evolution. Like the higher mental subplanes, these planes are accessed only through the doorway of the trained mind— the mind is the key.

THE BUDDHIC PLANE: THE KINGDOM OF GOD

The Buddhic plane is the plane of pure being. It is on this plane that the intuitional, or Christ, consciousness is fully developed. This plane is home to liberated souls who are no longer chained to the "wheel of rebirth." When we've reached this level of evolution, the causal body vanishes and our individual souls merge and become one with the universal spirit.

According to the Wisdom teachings, this level is home to the super-human beings who guide the evolution of our planet. Called the "Celestial Hierarchy" in the Bible (Col. 1:16), this group of "perfected men" have also been called the Occult Hierarchy, the Church Invisible, and the Great White Brotherhood. In ancient Egypt they were called the Immortals; in Persia, the Magi; in Babylon, the Great Ones.[19]

The more subtle version of our astral senses can be found on this plane. Clairvoyance becomes spiritual vision, the ability to see beyond the limitations of time and space. Sequential time, a function of our finite brains, disappears as we live in the Eternal Now. Psychometry becomes healing touch, the ability to heal through the laying on of hands, as illustrated by Jesus in the Gospel stories. Clairaudience becomes divine hearing, the ability to be in telepathic contact with angelic forms and spiritual masters.

Symbolized by air, this plane is called the *Mahar Prajapatya*, or the "Great World," in the Hindu scriptures; *Atzilut* in the kabbalah; and the "superconscious world" by the Sufis.

THE SPIRITUAL, OR ATMIC, PLANE

The spiritual plane, called *Jana* by the Hindus and "the realm of pure spirit" by the Sufis, is the plane of divine will. Here, the hidden divinity in man finds full expression. Also called *nirvana*, this is the plane of bliss, tranquility, and peace. When we reach this level of consciousness, our evolutionary journey is complete. The human being has become divine.

The final two planes—the monadic, the plane of God-consciousness; and the divine plane, the plane of "absolute consciousness"—are the planes of divine activity. According to the Wisdom teachings, the divine energies that circulate and sustain our solar system originate on these levels.

THE SEVEN KINGDOMS

The teaching on the seven kingdoms is especially significant to our evolutionary journey, as it illustrates our role in the so-called Great Plan for humanity.

The seven kingdoms include the mineral, vegetable, animal, human, spiritual, planetary, and solar kingdoms. With the three spiritual kingdoms above and the three subhuman kingdoms below, the human kingdom is the middle kingdom. Standing "where the two seas meet," we occupy the central place in the scheme of creation—the link between the spiritual and the material worlds.

The teaching on our role in this "great chain of being" can also be found in other spiritual traditions. Buddhism teaches that humans occupy "the middle realm" between animals and *asura*, the realm of *devas*, or "angels" and demi-gods. The kabbalah teaches that human beings are essential for *yechidut*, the unification of the higher and lower worlds.

Alice Bailey writes about the central place of the human being: "Above, we find the spiritual triplicity, below, a material triplicity and humanity—containing in itself the essence of both the higher and lower—must act as a transformer and a transmitter from the higher to the lower. This constitutes our service."[20]

When we build our bridge to the soul, the spiritual light above will flow through us to the three lower kingdoms. In linking the higher with the lower, we help the lower kingdoms to evolve. When, as Bailey put it, we "lift those kingdoms into heaven and bring heaven down to earth,"[21] the five kingdoms—mineral, vegetable, animal, human, and spiritual— will function on earth as one beautiful, vital, harmonious whole.

This event is the "marriage made in the Heavens" spoken of in the Old Testament (Gen. 2:24). According to the Wisdom teachings, this fusion—the establishment of the Kingdom of God on earth—is mankind's spiritual destiny. Saint Paul spoke of this destiny when he said, "The whole of creation waits with eager longing for the children of God to be revealed" (Rom 8:23).

THE SEVEN STREAMS

The Wisdom teachings tell us that there are seven specific stages in the growth and evolution of humanity. Called the "seven streams" in the Hindu scriptures and the seven "suns" or "worlds" in native cultures, each stream represents one of the seven developmental stages. In *The Secret Doctrine*, Blavatsky calls each stage a "root race." In this case, the word *race* refers to a specific stage, rather than a racial type.

Science tells us that modern man emerged in Africa one hundred thousand years ago. According to *The Secret Doctrine*, humans have existed on earth for millions of years—a view that can also be found in the Hindu spiritual texts. The *Puranas*, or "Histories," tell of human civilizations existing on this planet for tens of millions of years.

While researching this topic, I came across *Forbidden Archeology: The Hidden History of the Human Race*, by Michael Cremo and Richard Thompson. According to the authors, human skeletal remains and artifacts have been found in rock formations that date back millions of years. Their book, an eight-hundred-page review of archeological evidence from the 1800s to the present, makes a compelling argument for a prehistoric human presence on earth. After examining thousands of scientific documents, they concluded that the evidence not consistent with the modern theory of evolution has been systematically dismissed or suppressed.[22]

I like the esoteric teaching on the root races, as it illustrates the planned unfoldment, the slow step-by-step emergence of our full sensory capabilities. As we develop both our physical and subtle senses, we move slowly but surely from primitive life to the superhuman state of our great spiritual leaders.

Here again the seven races are divided into seven subraces. Each race is said to reach the peak of its achievement at the midpoint—the fourth or fifth subrace. From that point, the next subrace, the pioneers of the next evolutionary wave, are born.

The first three races represent the downward arc, the descent of spirit into matter. During this period, the emphasis is on building the physical body. On the upward arc, our bodies once again become lighter and more ethereal.

According to Blavatsky, the bodies of the first race were composed entirely of subtle matter. Ethereal and transparent, they were called the "mindless race" because the mind principle was dormant. The first root race developed the sense of hearing. The first race gradually merged into the second. This second race was semihuman, their bodies boneless and still largely etheric. The evolutionary purpose of this race was the development of the etheric body. Called Hyperboreans, they possessed a faint spark of mind and developed the sense of touch.

The greatest evolutionary leap occurred during the third root race. The purpose of this race was both the development of the human form and the awakening of the mind principle. This race, called *Danavas* in the Hindu texts, had ape-like bodies. Initially composed mostly of gases, liquids, and solids, they later developed a skeletal structure and the sense of sight. This race is said to represent the lowest descent of spirit into matter—our journey to the "far country," the biblical "fall" of mankind. It is here that we became individualized and seemingly separate.

During the fourth race, the upward arc, the evolutionary journey began. Called the Atlantean race, its evolutionary purpose was both the perfection of the physical form and the development of the emotional body. The Atlantean race developed the sense of taste and the psychic faculties—clairvoyance, clairaudience, psychometry—associated with the emotional body. In touch with subtle energies, they had the ability to control the elemental forces of nature. It is said that the abuse of these powers led to the great flood, mentioned in the Old Testament and other world scriptures, that submerged the continent of Atlantis.

The fifth and current root race is called the Aryan race. During this evolutionary cycle, the development of the mental body is the goal. Our race developed the last of the physical senses, the sense of smell. According to the Wisdom teachings, we live in the age of the fifth subrace, a time when the development of the lower mind has reached its peak. It is during our time that the seeds of the next evolutionary development—union with the soul—take root. It is also a time when the forerunners of the sixth race appear. Some believe the so-called "new children," a subject I will examine in chapter 3, are the first wave of this new race.

Not much is written about the two final stages. As in the earlier races, the last two will be more ethereal than physical. During the sixth race the widespread emergence of the higher mind is the goal. The Hindu scriptures describe this race has having minds as "clear as crystal."[23] According to Native American lore, our consciousness and civilization will be completely transformed during this "sixth sun" era. The kabbalists, who call this era the age of the messiah, also point to a profound shift in consciousness during this period.[24] According to Blavatsky, this race will appear in about four hundred years.[25]

Said to be "untold ages" into the future,[26] the development of the seventh sense—instant perception—will be the goal of the seventh race. According to Blavatsky, humans will become omniscient: space and time will disappear as the past, present, and future are experienced in each moment. Called the "cycle of jeweled splendor" in the Hindu texts, this race represents the final integration of soul and body and the perfection of this evolutionary cycle.[27]

YOGAS

It has been said that during each race, a specific practice is given to mankind to stimulate each new evolutionary development. These practices are called yogas. According to Willard Johnson in *Riding the*

Ox Home: A History of Meditation from Shamanism to Science, the word *yoga* comes from the root verb *yuj*, "to harness." Johnson writes that the original meaning of the word, usually translated as "union," has its basis in the achievement of a particular skill or ability.[28] With that in mind, it is easy to see how each type of yoga fits into the evolutionary scheme.

Hatha Yoga

As we've seen above, the third race was focused on the development and stabilization of the human form. The goal of hatha yoga, the yoga of the body, was the conscious control of the organs and muscles of the physical body.

Laya and Bhakti Yoga

Laya yoga, which focuses on the development of the energy centers, helped the Atlantean race to stabilize the energies of the etheric body. Laya yoga later gave way to the bhakti yoga, the yoga of devotion. This yoga emphasizes communion with God. The goal of bhakti yoga, focused on the heart and the feeling nature, is the control of the emotional body.

Raja Yoga

Raja, for "royal" or "kingly," is the yoga of the mind. The goal of this yoga is the conscious control of the mental body, the task of the fifth race. This yoga is called kingly, as the mastery of the mental body completes the development of the human personality. Once we gain conscious control over our physical, emotional, and mental bodies, we become a fit vehicle for the soul, or the God within.

Agni Yoga

Agni yoga, the yoga of the soul, is related to synthesis, our identification with the whole. Mastery of this still-emerging yoga is the task of the sixth root race and the pioneers of our time.

THE GREAT TURNING

We are experiencing "the great turning," the transition from one astrological age to the next. This transition is due to an astronomical phenomenon known as the precession of the equinoxes. *Precession* refers to the orbital motion of the earth; the slow and continuous shift in the earth's orientation is similar to a spinning top. As the earth revolves around the sun, the equinoxes move westward along the ecliptic and slowly pass through each constellation of the zodiac. The entire cycle, called a "great year," takes 25,800 years. Each age of roughly two thousand years is determined by the stars that rise with the sun on the day of the spring equinox. During each two-thousand-year period, we are influenced by the subtle energies that emanate from each constellation.

There is a lot of talk about the "end times" these days, and we are in fact living at the end of the current age of Pisces. Many dates have been given for the start of the Age of Aquarius—from the 1960s to the year 2000. I prefer to use the astronomical date 2376 for the dawn of this new age. This time period roughly corresponds to the first emergence of the sixth root race.

Students of astrology will be interested to note how the corresponding zodiac symbols pop up during each two-thousand-year period. The bull is the symbol associated with Taurus, and the Age of Taurus coincided with the bull-worshiping cults in Crete, Egypt,

Persia, and Rome. The founding of Judaism occurred during the Age of Aries; and the ram, the symbol associated with the sign of Aries, is the traditional Hebrew symbol of hope and strength. Christianity was established during the Piscean Age. The oldest symbol for this religion is the fish, the symbol associated with the sign of Pisces. Pisces is an otherworldly, emotional sign, and Jesus's teachings on love, compassion, and forgiveness have characterized the Piscean Age. The keynote of this period has been religion, mysticism, and devotion to spiritual leaders and gurus.

The zodiacal image for the sign of Aquarius is the water-bearer. The biblical verse, "Behold, when ye are entered into the city, there shall a man meet you, bearing a pitcher of water; follow him into the house where he entereth in" (Luke 22:10) is said to be a direct reference to the coming Age of Aquarius. In the same way that our focus of attention gradually moves from the emotional to the mental plane, in the Aquarian Age our focus will shift from the emotional nature to the mind, the doorway to the soul. Each age represents a higher turn on the spiral of evolution, and it is during the Age of Aquarius that direct contact with the soul will become widespread. Aquarius is a mental sign, and the ability to use the mind to "see" in two directions—outward into the physical world or upward into the subtle worlds—will increase. Telepathic communication will also become widespread.

During the Piscean Age, spiritual practice in the West has been largely *exoteric*—focused on scriptures, rituals, and church services. During the Aquarian Age, the exoteric practices will give way to esoteric, or inner, development. The other characteristics of this age will include the merging of science and mysticism and a revolution in education. Children will be taught to access information by intuitive means. Aquarius is the sign of brotherhood, and this era will also include the restoration of the mysteries teachings and the establish-ment of a one-world religion.

As we get closer to this doorway, the signs of this new era can be seen all around us as the old world disintegrates and a new, more inclusive and compassionate world slowly takes shape. In the next chapter we will look at the seven energy centers, with a special emphasis on the heart. I will show you how these centers relate to the evolutionary journey, higher levels of telepathic perception, and the creation of the new world.

Chapter Two

THE UNIVERSAL HUMAN

Heaven in its totality reflects a single person . . . and each
person is therefore called the universal human. . . . The
communities that make up heaven are arranged like the
members, organs, and viscera in a human being.

—Emanuel Swedenborg, *Heaven and Hell*

In *Emergence: The Shift from Ego to Essence*, Barbara Marx Hubbard defines a Universal Human as "one who is connected through the heart to the whole of life, attuned to the deeper intelligence of nature, and called forth irresistibly by spirit to creatively express his or her gifts in the evolution of self and the world." The Universal Human, Hubbard writes, is "one who has shifted identity from the ego to the deeper self that is a direct expression of Source." Like so many others today, Hubbard believes that we're on the cusp of an evolutionary leap. Those of us on earth today, Hubbard says, are "the cross-over generation, responsible for leading the way from one stage of our species' evolution to the next."[1]

According to the Wisdom tradition, our evolutionary shift from the personal to the universal comes about through the gradual awakening of our higher energy centers. In Eastern spiritual traditions, these energy centers are called *chakras*, a Sanskrit word that translates as "wheel" or "vortex." The centers, allied with the seven senses, run parallel to the spine, from the base to the top of the head. In Buddhist art, they are depicted as lotuses drawn on the foot, the palm of the hand, and other areas of the body. As stated in the previous chapter, the centers are located in the etheric, not the physical, body.

This teaching is also part of the Western spiritual tradition. In Egypt, each of the temples and monuments along the Nile River—including the twin temples of Ramses and his queen, Nefertari; the temple of Hathor; and the Great Pyramid—is said to symbolize one of these seven centers.[2] The centers are also part of the esoteric teachings of the Rosicrucians, the Freemasons, and the Theosophists.

Each of the major glands of the endocrine system—the adrenals, gonads, pancreas, thymus, thyroid, pituitary body, and pineal gland—is linked to an energy center. The three centers below the diaphragm—the basic center, associated with the adrenals; the sacral center, associated with the gonads; and the solar plexus, associated with the pancreas—form a triangle symbolizing the earth, or matter, aspect. These three centers govern the personal, seemingly separate self. They represent our instinctive, animal nature: the instinct of sex and self-preservation, and our emotional reactions and personal attachments to others. The four centers above the diaphragm—the heart, throat, and two head centers—form a triangle of spiritual energies. Together, the two triangles represent both the higher and lower aspects of our nature.

In most of humanity today, only the lower three centers are fully functional. We are living in a time when the all-important heart center is starting to unfold. Since I'll be referring to them later, I've included a brief look at the esoteric teaching on the seven centers below. Within this teaching is the story of our spiritual evolution. Each center is a doorway into a new, more subtle world and a higher level of telepathic perception.

THE BASIC CENTER

Located at the base of the spine, the basic center supports the other six by providing the will to live, the fundamental instinct of self-preservation. It is here that the kundalini, universally known as the "serpent of God," lies dormant until activated by the evolutionary process. In Sanskrit, this center is called *muladhara,* or "root," to symbolize the gravitational force that keeps us anchored to the earth.

THE SACRAL CENTER

Linked to our reproductive organs, this center is the source of our sexuality and vitality. Since this center relates to the creative process of reproduction, it is linked with the throat, or creative, center. As we grow spiritually, the energies of the sacral center are gradually transferred to the throat. When this energy is transmuted, our creative ideas and projects take the place of physical reproduction.

THE SOLAR PLEXUS

Like the other two centers below the diaphragm, the solar plexus center plays a major part in our personal lives. This is the center of emotion, the instinctive love and attachment we feel for our mates, families, and friends. It is also the center of personal ambition and desire—for love, money, status, and even our own spiritual fulfillment.

Connected to the emotional body, the solar plexus center is often referred to as the instinctual brain. This is the center of psychic sensitivity and mediumship, a subject we will look at more closely in chapter 4. As we develop spiritually, the energies of the solar plexus are gradually transmuted; spiritual living and thinking creates a "pull" that moves the energy of the solar plexus into the heart.

THE HEART CENTER

The heart center, linked to the thymus gland, is located behind the physical heart. With three material centers below and three spiritual centers above, this center represents the borderline between the visible and the invisible worlds. When the heart center opens, a profound shift begins. The personal now becomes universal; we lose our sense of separateness and draw closer to our souls. Our personal emotions give way to universal love. Our selfish desire, our personal ambition, now becomes a desire to work for the greater good. The Bible says that "the love of God is shed abroad in the human heart" (Rom. 5:5); and, as I'll demonstrate below, this step is necessary for the creation of the new world.

We are connected to our souls by two energetic threads. The first, called the life thread, is anchored in the heart center. The soul brings life to the body through the heart and blood stream.

THE THROAT CENTER

The throat center is the first to open when our energies move above the diaphragm. This center is very active in today's spiritual seekers. When the creative energy of the sacral center moves to the throat center, it registers the creative impulse of the soul. When the throat center is open, we can bring inspiration to the world through our creative work—our writing, speaking, painting, or music. Its location covers an area behind the back of the neck, extending to the ears and down toward the shoulder blades. Its physical counterpart is the thyroid gland.

THE AJNA CENTER

The *ajna* center is located slightly above and between the eyes. It is called the "throne between the eyebrows" in the Hindu texts. Also called the third eye, this center is related to our lower mind and psychic functions. When developed, it expresses the intelligence of the fully integrated personality. Its physical counterpart is the pituitary gland.

THE HEAD CENTER

Located at the top of the head, this center is called the "thousand-petalled lotus," or the *Brahmarandra* in the Hindu texts. This center is related to the intuitive mind and our higher mental facilities. Its physical counterpart is the pineal gland. This gland sits in the center of the brain, behind and above the pituitary gland. Called the "seat of the soul" by Descartes, the French philosopher and mathematician, this is the point where the soul and body meet. The consciousness thread, the second thread that connects our bodies to the soul, is anchored in the region of this gland. This thread, called the *sutratma* in the Hindu texts and the "silver cord" in the Bible, provides a direct link between the soul and the physical brain.

In India, a yogi with an awakened head center is called a *Paramahansa*, or "Great Swan," due, some believe, to the bird-like shape of the lateral ventricles in the upper brain. Kabir, a fifteenth-century Indian mystic and poet, illustrated this experience in the following poem:

> O Swan, awake, arise, follow me.
> There is a land where doubt nor sorrow have rule;
> where the terror of death is no more.
> There the woods of spring are a-bloom,
> and the fragrant scent of "He is I"
> is borne on the wind:
> There, the bee of the heart is deeply immersed
> and desires no other joy.[3]

The pituitary and pineal glands—called "evolutionary sleepers" by one author[4]—are our keys to the higher worlds. Their higher functions remain dormant until activated by the inflow of energy from the soul. The flow of soul energy to the brain awakens new brain cells and stimulates our optic nerve, which makes it possible to register the etheric realm. Eventually, this downflow will result in a light, both within and around the head—a light so bright that it can look like a halo, as in pictures of the Christ and other religious figures.

When the head center is open, the kundalini rises from the base of the spine. This leads to the final integration of soul and body, what the Bible calls being "raised into Heaven" (Eph. 2:6). The serpent pictured on the brows of the Egyptian pharaohs depicted this state of consciousness. This stage of "perfected humanity" is the goal of the seventh race.

The Seven Seals

I've come across several interesting commentaries on the book of Revelation by well-known figures such as Edgar Cayce, D. H. Lawrence, and Swami Sri Yukteswar, best known through the writings of his student, Paramahansa Yogananda. These authors equate the seven seals in the book of Revelation with the seven centers above. In this symbolic book, the centers are variously referred to as the seven seals, the seven golden candlesticks, and the seven churches.

In his commentary on the book of Revelation, D. H. Lawrence writes, "The famous book of seven seals . . . is the body of man . . . of Adam; and of any man. . . . And the seven seals are the seven centers. . . . We are witnessing the opening and conquest of the great psychic centers of the human body. The old Adam is going to be conquered, die, and reborn as the new Adam. But in stages. In seven stages, or in six stages and then a climax, seven."[5] The book of Revelation is usually read as an apocalyptic tale about the final battle between good and evil. The literal meaning of the word *apocalypse*, derived from the Greek word *apokalypsis*, is "unveiling" or "revealing." The true battle between good and evil—between our lower and higher natures—happens within. When our higher centers are fully awakened, the energies of divine love will flow through us from the spiritual kingdom to the subhuman worlds. When the spiritual and physical worlds are united, the "new heaven and a new earth," mentioned in Revelation, will be revealed.

Transhumanism

While researching this chapter, I read several articles on transhumanism, a movement that started in the 1980s. The goal of this movement is the merging of humans with advanced computer technology. By adding advanced computer components to our brains and bodies, transhumanists believe that we can enhance our intellectual and physical capacities, transcend our biological limitations, and create a new species they call the "posthuman."

In the New Testament, Jesus said, "ye will be Gods" (John 10:34); and, like an acorn, the potential of growth is already within us. We are born with all the "hardware" we'll ever need—hardware that is slowly activated by the evolutionary process. We need only to unveil the faculties we already possess to reach the superhuman or posthuman state.

OPENING THE HEART

It is not without reason that the Teaching of the Heart is so needed for the life of the future. Otherwise, how shall you cross the boundaries of the Worlds?

—Helena Roerich[6]

It is in heart that we first contact the soul and cross the boundary between the worlds. This is an essential step for all evolutionary pioneers. Opening the heart, author Thomas Merton says, is the true beginning, the necessary preparation that makes us ready for the work "which eye hath not seen, and ear hath not heard . . . the work that God revealed in the Bible."[7] Its central role in spiritual development is illustrated in this fable:

A hermit emerged from his solitude with a message, saying to each person he met, "Thou possesseth a heart." When he was asked why he did not speak of mercy, of patience, devotion, and other beneficent foundations of life, he answered, "The heart alone must not be forgotten; the rest will come."[8]

Higher development without an open heart can lead to the dangerous, egocentric behavior we've seen in dictators and other world leaders. The need for an open heart is one of the "eternal verities," an ageless truth expressed in the following biblical verse: "If I speak with the tongues of men and of angels, but do not have love, I have become a noisy gong or a clanging cymbal. If I have the gift of prophecy, and know all mysteries and all knowledge; and if I have all faith, so as to remove mountains, but do not have love, I am nothing" (1 Cor. 13:1).

The sun is the center of our solar system, and in the same way, the heart is the center of our own individual universe. For this reason, the esoteric teaching on the heart was called "sun-knowledge" in the ancient world. The Egyptians were among the first to record their beliefs about the heart. For the Egyptians, the heart was the supreme organ in the body, an instrument of the Divine, the source of life and being. It was through the heart that they heard the words of God. During the embalming process, the heart was the only organ left in the body. After death, the virtue of the deceased was judged in a ceremony called the "trial of the heart."

This ceremony is depicted in a series of papyri in the Egyptian Book of the Dead, a collection of ancient funereal texts. These images show the jackal-headed god Anubis, the judge of the dead, with a large scale. The scale is balanced on the left end by an urn symbolizing the heart of the deceased. On the right side of the scale is an ostrich feather, the symbol of truth and justice. If the heart was lighter than the feather, the deceased was judged to be virtuous and permitted to live with the Gods "in eternal life and bliss." If the heart was heavier, it was thought to be weighted down by sin and immediately eaten by a monster—part crocodile, part hippopotamus, and part lion—called the "eater of the dead." Without the heart, which was associated with the *ka*, or "soul," the deceased was condemned to "eternal oblivion."[9]

In many cultures, the heart center is the key to healing. The Chinese consider the heart to be "the emperor of the human body." The *Huang Di nei jing su wen*, the seminal medical text of ancient China, states that "the heart holds the office of lord and sovereign. The radiance of the spirits stems from it." The Chinese also believe the heart to be the home of the *shen*. The shen are the messengers of heaven, "the principle of life, that which transforms an assemblage of matter into a living being."[10]

The Japanese also place great emphasis on the heart. In the Shinto tradition, the qualities of a bright heart, a pure heart, a correct heart, and a straight heart are necessary to achieve harmony with the gods. Together, these qualities create a state of purity known as *seimei shin*. The Japanese also consider *ishin-denshin*, or "harmony between hearts," to be the highest priority in relationships. In the Japanese dictionary, the entry for *ishin-denshin* is cross-referenced with *isshin-dōtai*, a term defined as "one heart, the same body," indicating a deep feeling of connection between two people.[11]

The African Bushmen also believe that they are connected to others through the heart. In *The Heart of the Hunter*, Sir Laurens van der Post writes of his journey through the Kalahari Desert to document the lives of the Bushmen. One night, asleep in the desert, his Bushman interpreter woke him up with the news that people in trouble were coming their way. When asked how he knew, he tapped his chest and said, "I can feel it in here." Soon after, a group of wandering Bushmen appeared, desperate for food and water.[12]

It is in the heart that the soul first makes its presence known in the still, small voice of conscience; and, in many traditions, the word *heart* is synonymous with *soul*. Christians use the term *Christ consciousness* to describe the soul, the master in the heart— what Saint Paul called "the Christ in you, the hope of glory" (Col 1:27). The Upanishads, a collection of Vedic texts, state that Brahma "always dwells in the heart of man as the supreme soul. Those who realize him through the immediate perception of the heart attain immortality." In the Agni Yoga tradition, the heart is called "the abode of God." The heart, we are told, does not belong to us; it is given from above. It is referred to as "an international organ, a vessel of universal energy."

In *Hierarchy*, Helena Roerich has written, "What is the treasure of the heart? Not only well-wishing; not only compassion; not only devotion . . . but consonance with the cosmic consciousness, when the heart, beside its own rhythm, even partakes in the cosmic rhythm. Such a heart may be trusted; it possesses straight-knowledge; it feels and knows, and as a manifested link with the higher world, it expresses the indisputable."[13]

When we open our hearts, we see divinity all around us: in the beauty of the vivid colors on a sunny fall day, or the sweetness in a stranger's eyes as we push our shopping cart around the grocery store.

VIRTUES OF THE HEART

In the Wisdom teachings, the heart is known as the twelve-petaled lotus; each petal is said to embody the virtues or qualities that the heart is destined to express: selflessness, humility, service, labor, patience, tolerance, spiritual identification, compassion, sympathy, wisdom, sacrifice, and gratitude. As we develop the virtues of the heart, the petals open one by one and, eventually, a beautiful chalice, the "jewel in the lotus," is revealed.

In Buddhism, there are ten "perfections," or virtues, of the heart. Of these virtues—generosity, integrity, simplicity, wisdom, strength, patience, truthfulness, determination, lovingkindness, and equanimity—the Buddha considered the ninth, lovingkindness, to be the most important. In his famous sermon on lovingkindness he stated that "meditations and religious exercises pacify the heart, comprehension of the truth leads to Nirvana, but greater than all is lovingkindness. As the light of the moon is sixteen times stronger than the light of all the stars, so lovingkindness is sixteen times more efficacious in liberating the heart than all other religious accomplishments taken together. This state of heart is the best in the world."[14]

An open heart has a magnetic power that affects all who come into contact with it. Many who have met the Dalai Lama in person have commented on the love and compassion he radiates. The Dalai Lama, who has said that "kindness is my religion," has stated that "there is no need for temples; no need for complicated philosophy. Our own brain, our own heart is our temple; the philosophy is kindness."[15]

The virtues of the heart are cultivated by the spiritual disciplines of meditation and service. Cultivating these virtues creates the spiritual "pull" that brings our energies up from the solar plexus. Below are meditations on lovingkindness and altruistic joy, two of the sublime states taught by the Buddha. Done regularly, these meditations will help you to open your heart. I will also introduce you to two additional heart-opening meditations in chapter 5. I adapted these meditations from those taught by the spiritual healer Steven Lumiere and the Buddhist scholar Jack Kornfield.

MEDITATION ON LOVINGKINDNESS

I think of this meditation as a daily prayer for the health and happiness of others—and myself.

Give yourself fifteen minutes of uninterrupted quiet time. Calm yourself by closing your eyes and following your breath, in and out, for a count of ten.

1. When you're ready, think of someone you love—a mate, parent, child, or beloved friend. Feel your love for them, and project that love from your heart to their heart. As you do, inwardly recite these words: "May you be happy; may you be well." Imagine these words as a blessing that will positively affect each person's day. Repeat this process with each of your loved ones in turn.

2. When you've finished, feel and project lovingkindness to yourself and inwardly recite, "May I be filled with lovingkindness; may I be happy; may I be well." As you do, imagine that your heart is opening a little more each day and that your love for yourself and others is steadily increasing.

3. Feel and project lovingkindness to anyone with whom you have difficulties. As you inwardly recite the prayer, imagine that your words are, little by little, dissolving any ill will, anger, or resentment between you. Repeat this process as many times as necessary.

4. Feel and project lovingkindness toward the other people in your world: your friends, neighbors, and coworkers.

5. Feel and project lovingkindness toward all the people on earth. If it feels right to you, you can focus your attention on specific, hard-hit areas where people are suffering from the effects of famine, war, or natural disasters.

6. Feel and project lovingkindness toward everything on the earth; the plants, animals, and even the earth itself.

Meditation on Altruistic Joy

Altruistic joy is the ability to rejoice at the good fortune of others. This meditation is fun; you will use your powers of visualization to help others to create their heart's desire. It will also help you eliminate feelings of envy and jealousy over the success or prosperity of others.

Give yourself fifteen minutes of uninterrupted quiet time. Calm yourself by closing your eyes and following your breath, in and out, for a count of ten.

1. When you're ready, think of someone you love—a mate, parent, child, or beloved friend. Think about their heart's desire: is it a wonderful relationship, the successful completion of a creative project, or a deepening sense of peace and fulfillment? Imagine that person receiving this wonderful gift and, as you do, inwardly recite this prayer: "May you be joyful; may your happiness increase." Feel the joy within you as you see your loved one happy and content. Repeat this process with each of your loved ones.

2. When you've finished, take a moment to imagine that you have received your heart's desire and inwardly say, "May I be joyful; may my happiness increase." Feel the joy you'll experience when this gift arrives.

3. Feel and project altruistic joy to anyone with whom you have difficulties. Imagine that they have received their heart's desire— even if you're not sure what that desire is—and, as you do, inwardly recite the prayer, "May you be joyful; may your happiness increase." Repeat this step as many times as necessary.

4. Feel and project altruistic joy toward the other people in your world: friends, neighbors, or coworkers. Imagine that they have all received their heart's desire; picture them feeling happy and content.

5. Feel and project altruistic joy toward all the people on earth. If it feels right to you, you can focus your attention on a specific area. Imagine that the people who have been suffering from a lack of food, the effects of war, or a natural disaster are now getting exactly what they need to be happy and well.

6. Feel and project altruistic joy toward *everything* on the earth: the plants, the animals, and even the earth itself.

THE UNIFIED HEART

Anyone who has ever attended Sunday school has heard a lot about the Second Coming, the moment when Jesus will return to earth. The Wisdom teachings tell us that this event—known as the return of the Messiah, the Maitreya, the Bodhisattva, or the Imam Mahdi in other traditions—will occur when our heart centers bloom. It is when our hearts are opened and aligned with one another that the path of return is created.

The French philosopher Pierre Teilhard de Chardin, who spoke on the need for the "unification" of human hearts, has said, "The day will come when, after harnessing the winds, the tides and gravitation, we shall harness for God the energies of Love. And on that day, for the second time in the history of the world, man will have discovered fire."[16]

As all the great spiritual traditions tell us, the path of knowledge must be added to the path of love. In the next chapter, I will introduce you to the Wisdom teachings on the three aspects of the mind.

Chapter Three

THE THREE MINDS

The seer is pure vision . . . he looks out
through the medium of the mind.

—Patanjali, *The Yoga Sutras*

In this chapter, I will cover the Ageless Wisdom teachings on the mind in more detail, show you how this teaching appears in other spiritual traditions, and introduce you to the science that is now validating this ancient wisdom.

THE TRUE SIXTH SENSE

Called the *rajah*, or "king," of the senses, the mind is said to be our true sixth sense, the synthesis of our other five senses. As I mentioned in the introduction, our minds are designed to work in two directions—outward onto the physical plane and upward into the subtle worlds of pure spirit. Just as we use our eyes to see on the physical plane, the trained mind becomes the tool we use to "see" on the subtle planes.

The Wisdom teachings tell us that there are three aspects to the mind—the lower, rational mind; the soul, our individual fragment of the divine mind; and the higher, or intuitive, mind. The lower mind, linked to our five physical senses, is the reasoning principle. We use this aspect of the mind to function in the physical world. The higher mind is the custodian of abstract ideas and universal concepts. When we tap this level of mind, we have access to the universal, or divine, mind—the great storehouse of all wisdom and knowledge. It is the soul that connects the two minds. This bridging occurs on the mental plane, as I outlined in chapter 1.

When the mind is focused outward, it telegraphs information about the physical world to our brains. This information is transmitted through the avenue of our five physical senses—we hear, see, touch, taste, and smell the world around us. When the physical senses are stilled through meditation, the mind turns inward and upward. When the mind is focused upward, it functions as a conduit, transferring information from the soul to the brain.

Our rational minds cannot make direct contact with the subtle planes. It is only through the soul that we have access to divine ideas and concepts. This fact is illustrated in a famous painting called *Medencolia I* by the sixteenth-century German artist and lifelong student of the Ageless Wisdom, Albrecht Durer. In this painting, a brooding figure sits surrounded by symbols of the human intellect: measuring scales, an hourglass, and a variety of geometric solids. As Dan Brown points out in *The Lost Symbol*, these objects represent the failure of the human mind to directly register enlightened ideas and spiritual truths.

When the soul brings the higher and lower minds into alignment, information on all subjects becomes possible. We have access to divine ideas and universal truths once available only to a gifted few. The Greeks use the word *gnosis*, from *nous*, or "mind," to describe this experience. According to Richard Smoley, *nous* was defined in an eighteenth-century text as "the highest faculty in man, through which . . . he knows God. . . . The intellect . . . understands divine truth by means of immediate experience, intuition, or 'simple cognition.'"[1]

As I will show you in chapter 6, it is through meditation that we create the threads and cables that connect the three aspects of the mind. In the same way that our homes are wired for phone and internet reception, these threads function as communication lines that allow us to receive information from the higher planes. Over time, as we project our attention upward, these threads and cables fuse and widen as a symbolic bridge between the physical and spiritual worlds is built. This bridge is built in two pieces. The lower span links the lower mind and the soul. When we build this bridge, we create a direct channel for the downpouring of information from the soul to the brain, where it is interpreted and used. As you'll see in the next chapter, this experience has produced many of our greatest achievements in religion, the arts, and business.

At a later stage in our spiritual development, the higher span—the one between the soul and the higher mind—is built. We then have a direct link between the higher mind and the brain, an experience that prompted Jesus to say, "I and my Father are one." When the three minds unite, we have access to all information—past, present, and future. Time and space disappear as the past, present, and future are experienced in each moment. According to the Wisdom teachings, this bridge building is the "new and true" science of the mind.[2]

EAST AND WEST

As you'll see below, this teaching lies at the heart of both the Eastern and Western spiritual traditions. As I've mentioned in the introduction, the Hindu sage Patanjali, founder of the raja yoga school, was the first to put the Wisdom teachings on the mind into book form. The dates of his birth and death are unknown, but most Western writers believe he lived somewhere between the years 820 and 300 BCE. The Hindus give even earlier dates—as far back as 10,000 BCE.[3]

Patanjali's book, *The Yoga Sutras*, is the foundational text of raja yoga, the yoga of the mind. This book consists of four sections, or "books," detailing the nature, purpose, and function of the mind. Patanjali called the mind an "organ of vision and transmission,"[4] an instrument of the soul. It is through the practice of Raja Yoga, Patanjali wrote, that the brain can register the wisdom of the soul.

In the first section of *The Yoga Sutras*, Patanjali provides instructions for quieting the mind and emotions. In the second, he includes practices for contacting the soul. The third section focuses on mind control and the need to develop a one-pointed focus of attention, and the fourth covers the stage of universal consciousness.

A more recent teaching on the mind can be found in the work of Sri Aurobindo, a twentieth-century Hindu master. Aurobindo also teaches that the next evolution in nature is our transition from human intelligence to superconscious awareness. In *The Life Divine* and other books, he presents his teaching on the mind. Aurobindo's model includes four, rather than three, levels of mind. Aurobindo writes that the first step beyond the rational mind is the higher, or abstract, mind. The second is the illumined mind, which he calls "the mind of light" or "vision." The third is the intuitive mind, and the fourth is the divine or "supermind"—the level of cosmic consciousness where "the ego-sense is subordinated, lost in the largeness of being . . . a wide cosmic perception and the feeling of a boundless universal self replaces it."[5]

The teachings on the mind are also central to the practice of Buddhism. Students are told, "When you realize your own mind you will become a Buddha; you should not seek Buddhahood elsewhere." Their scriptures make a distinction between two types of mind: the rational, or conceptual, mind and the nonconceptual, or wisdom, mind, also referred to as the "buddha nature." Their scriptures also make a distinction between three levels of mental awareness—the gross mind, the subtle mind, and the very subtle mind. The gross, or conceptual, mind is our day-to-day waking mind. We access *alaya*, the subtle mind, when we sleep and dream. The very subtle mind, called *rigpa*, is the root, or universal, mind. Also called the "mind of clear light," this nonconceptual mind is accessed through deep meditation. Tapping into this level of mind gives us the pristine awareness of the Tibetan lamas, who are said to receive direct teachings from the Buddha by a process they call "pure vision."

In the Bible we are told, "Let the mind be in you, which was also in Christ Jesus" (Phil. 2:5). This teaching is also mentioned numerous times in the gnostic Gospels.

In the Gospel of Mary, a gnostic text found in Egypt in 1896, Mary describes to the other disciples the secret teaching on the mind she received from Jesus after the resurrection:

> I saw the Lord in a vision and I said to him, "Lord, I saw you today in a vision."
>
> He answered me, "Blessed are you for not wavering at seeing me. For where the mind is, there is the treasure."
>
> I said to him, "So now, Lord, does a person who sees a vision see it [with] the soul [or] with the spirit?"
>
> The Savior answered, "A person does not see with the soul or with the spirit. Rather the mind, which exists between these two, sees the vision."[6]

In another gnostic text, called the Testimony of Truth, the author advises those who have the ability to hear with "spiritual rather than physical ears" to go within and become "disciples of their [higher] minds," as the mind is "the father of truth."[7]

In the Secret Book of James, which some scholars believe was written as a sequel to the opening scene in the New Testament Acts, Jesus's brother James writes of the experience he and Peter had of "seeing with their minds" after Jesus ascended: "Peter and I gave thanks and sent our hearts upward toward heaven. . . . And when we had passed beyond that place, we sent our minds farther upward and saw with our eyes and heard with our ears . . . angels rejoicing, as we too, rejoiced."[8]

In the gnostic gospel entitled Discourse on the Eighth and Ninth, written as a dialog between a teacher called "Trismegistus" and his student, the teacher describes the experience of making contact with the divine mind, the mind of God:

> I see! I see indescribable depth. How shall I tell you, O my son? . . . How [shall I describe] the universe? I [am mind] and I see another mind, the one that [moves] the soul! . . . I have found the beginning of the power that is above all powers, the one that has no beginning. . . . I have said, O my son, that I am Mind. I have seen! Language is not able to reveal this . . . the angels sing a hymn in silence. And I, Mind, understand.[9]

Teachings on the mind can also be found in the Sufi and kabalistic traditions. *Kabbalah*, a Hebrew word meaning "to receive," is the esoteric branch of Judaism. In the kabbalah, the intuitive mind is called *chokhmah*, a level of consciousness defined as "pure, nonverbal, undifferentiated thought."[10] The early kabbalists left meditation manuals that described the mantras, breathing exercises, and body movements they used to access this level of mind. David Cooper tells us that Moses Cordovero, a sixth-century kabbalist, wrote of ancient Jewish mystics who had "special methods of concentration

. . . that strengthened their subtle minds in such a way as to appre-
hend the sublime, heavenly realms." Cooper mentions another early
sage who wrote of meditation practices that would allow one to have
visions of God and the ability to "look into his [own] mind like one
who reads a book in which are written great wonders."[11]

Sufism—from the words *suf*, meaning "wool," for the robes worn
by the early mystics; and *safa*, meaning "purity"—is the esoteric
branch of Islam. The ultimate goal of this spiritual tradition, as in
those mentioned above, is the perfection, or "completion," of the
human mind. The Sufis make contact with the subtle world by tapping into a level of mind they call ʿaql mujarrad, or "pure intellect."
According to Ibn ʿArabi, a thirteenth-century Sufi mystic and philosopher, "When a man has transformed himself into pure intellect
. . . he witnesses things that are the very source of what appears in
natural form. And he comes to know by intuitive knowledge how and
why the things of nature are just as they are."[12]

The Sufi poet Rumi commented on the higher levels of mind
this way:

> From realm to realm man went, reaching his present reasoning,
> knowledgeable, robust state—forgetting earlier forms of intelligence.
>   So, too, shall he pass beyond the current forms of perception. . . .
> There are a thousand other forms of Mind.[13]

Rumi also described his experience of the subtle worlds:

> The hidden world has its clouds and rain, but of a different kind.
> Its sky and sunshine are of a different kind.
> This is made apparent only to the refined ones—those not deceived
> by the seeming completeness of the ordinary world.[14]

QUANTUM MIND

What can science tell us about the higher functions of the mind? As you'll see below, the views of quantum scientists sound remarkably similar to the Ageless Wisdom teachings.

In *Infinite in All Directions*, physicist Freeman Dyson writes about his views of the mind:

> The universe shows evidence of . . . mind on three levels. The first is the level of elementary physical processes . . . the second level . . . is the level of direct human experience. There is evidence . . . that the universe as a whole is hospitable to the growth of mind . . . therefore, it is reasonable to believe in the existence of a third level of mind, a mental component of the universe. If we believe in this mental component of the universe, then we can say that we are small pieces of God's mental apparatus.[15]

Dyson's description of the final level is similar to that of the soul mentioned above.

Many pioneers of quantum science described the energetic web underlying matter as a "mind-like" sea of energy or an "information field." This view was shared by David Bohm, one of the great physicists of the last century. In *The Undivided Universe*, Bohm writes of "a mind-like quality present in every particle. . . . As we go to subtler levels, this mind-like quality becomes stronger and more developed." Bohm also believed the mind itself to be capable of "indefinitely greater levels of subtlety." He imagined the subtle levels of the mind as finely woven nets capable of "catching" ever more refined and subtle levels of information.[16]

Like C. G. Jung, many quantum scientists believe in the existence of a collective consciousness or group mind. According to Dossey, Erwin Schrödinger, who was greatly influenced by Eastern philosophy, was among the first to refer to the mind as "nonlocal"—not fixed within the brain of each individual.[17] Schrödinger called this collective mind the "One Mind." In his 1958 book, *Mind and Matter*, Schrödinger writes, "The multiplicity [of minds] is only apparent, in truth there is only one mind."[18] Bohm, too, wrote of a collective mind and pondered an even more comprehensive level of mind capable of extending "beyond the human species."[19]

In the 1920s, a Russian scientist named Vladimir Vernadsky introduced the term *noosphere*, from the Greek word *nous*, to describe his concept of the collective mind. His idea was further developed by Pierre Teilhard de Chardin, who considered the noosphere to be the "planetary thinking network" created by the interaction of human minds.[20]

Rupert Sheldrake and Dean Radin are two contemporary scientists who are continuing to explore the concept of a collective consciousness or group mind. Dean Radin is a senior scientist at the Institute of Noetic Sciences. In his book *Entangled Minds, Extrasensory Experiences in a Quantum Reality*, Radin ponders the "new reality" revealed by quantum science and describes the experience of living in an interconnected or "entangled" world:

> At a level of reality deeper than the ordinary senses can grasp, our brains and minds are in intimate communion with the universe. It is as though we live in a gigantic bowl of clear jello. Every wiggle—every movement, event and thought . . . is felt throughout the entire bowl. Except that this particular form of jello is a rather peculiar medium, in that it's not localized in the usual way. . . . It extends beyond the bounds of ordinary spacetime, and it's not even a substance in the usual sense of that word.[21]

This view sounds very similar to my description of the etheric web in chapter 1. Radin's latest book, *Supernormal: Science, Yoga, and the*

Evidence for Extraordinary Psychic Abilities, is a scientific look at the mental powers Patanjali describes in *The Yoga Sutras*.

Rupert Sheldrake first introduced his concept of an information field called a "morphic field" in the 1980s. In his book, *The Sense of Being Stared At and Other Aspects of the Extended Mind*, Sheldrake presents his theory that our minds form part of a collective "mental field" that is anchored in the brain but extends far beyond it. As he explains, "Through mental fields, the extended mind reaches out into the environment . . . this invisible connection links us to each other and the world around us."[22]

THE BRAIN: THE "DIVINE RECEIVER"

While most mainstream scientists make no distinction between the mind and the brain, the Wisdom teachings tell us that the brain is the externalization of the mind in the same way that our other organs—thyroid, stomach, and spleen, for example—are externalizations of the seven energy centers, or chakras.

Often called a "computer made of meat," the brain, with ten billion neurons, is the most complex organ in the body. According to the Wisdom teachings, the brain is designed to respond to stimuli from both the physical and subtle worlds. Called "divine receivers" by some, our brains are sophisticated receiving stations, capable of picking up a wide range of information, from the lowest planes to the highest. Like the mind, the brain has a dual function. The upper brain, in the region of the pineal gland, is the seat of intuitive perception; and the lower brain, in the region of the pituitary body, is the seat of emotion and concrete thinking. When we quiet the mind through meditation, the brain becomes still and receptive, ready to receive the inflow of information from the soul.

As I mentioned in the last chapter, when information from the soul flows into the brain, both the pineal and pituitary glands are activated. The downpouring energy from the soul has an effect on the physical structure of the brain, making it easier, over time, to register information from the subtle planes.

In *The Wonder of the Brain*, Gopi Krishna, a Hindu spiritual teacher, writes about the effect of higher states on the brain: "Since the brain is indispensable for all our activity . . . it is inconceivable that our consciousness can take a leap beyond its normal periphery without affecting its substance in any way. There is no historical precedent of a higher animal—say, a horse—ever attaining the mental stature of a human being, and co-mingling with other humans. . . . How can it then be possible for a human being to consort with gods without some kind of change in the brain?"[23]

In the last ten years, neuroscientists have studied the effect of contemplative practices on the brain. Their research has confirmed that mental training can and does bring about observable changes in our brains. In *How God Changes Your Brain*, neuroscientist Andrew Newberg describes the neurological changes associated with higher states of consciousness: "If you contemplate God long enough, something surprising happens in the brain. Neural functioning begins to change. Different circuits become activated, while others become deactivated. New dendrites are formed, new synaptic connections are made, and the brain becomes more sensitive to subtle realms of experience."[24]

Rick Hanson, a neuropsychologist and the author of *Buddha's Brain*, has also written about the effect of higher states on the brain.

As Hanson puts it, "Mental activity leaves lasting marks on the brain—much like a spring shower leaves tracks on a hillside . . . as neurons wire together, structure builds in the brain."[25]

Science tells us that the brain evolved from the tiny, primitive fish brain to the instinctive brain of the reptile, to the more sophisticated brain of the early mammal. In the mammal, the cerebral cortex grew and eventually dominated the primitive, reptilian brain. The growth of the cerebral cortex continued with the appearance of the monkey, the ape, and early man, eventually culminating in the intelligent human being.

Most scientists believe the evolution of the brain ended with the appearance of modern man. Practioners of the Ageless Wisdom tradition, as well as many neuroscientists and other researchers, believe our brains are continuing to evolve. In *The Biology of Transcendence: A Blueprint of the Human Spirit*, the renowned author Joseph Chilton Pearce makes his case for the continued evolution of the brain. He includes pictures of two toddlers with pronounced prefrontal lobes. In these pictures, the foreheads of both toddlers clearly extend beyond the tip of their noses. According to Pearce, a larger forebrain indicates increased capacity for intelligence, empathy, and compassion. While he has no figures on the number of children born with this brain configuration, Pearce believes these children to be an evolutionary response to our need for increased levels of intelligence and spiritual insight.[26]

In the last fifteen years, there has been a flood of books on the so-called indigo children. These children, born after 1980, are also said to have more pronounced frontal lobes. Other traits include increased sensitivity and intuitive ability, the ability to think abstractly, and brains that process information in unusual ways. These children are being diagnosed with ADD and ADHD in large numbers, and many need medication to function in our current educational system. Could their brains be more attuned to receiving information by intuitive means—rather than learning by rote?

People with autism represent the highest end of the sensitivity spectrum. According to William Stillman, author of *Autism and the God Connection* and other books on this subject, autistic people have a unique openness to the subtle realms. Stillman, who offers workshops and private consultations for individuals and families, has observed that autistic kids have pronounced intuitive abilities—precognition, telepathy, and the ability to communicate with animals and deceased loved ones. According to researchers, young children with autism also have larger brains and less insulation within the cortex. This lack of insulation makes it harder to block sensory input.[27]

Neurologist James Austin, author of *Zen and Brain,* has also researched the effects of meditation practices on the brain. When he lectures on the topic, he often shows slides of the Buddha with a top-knot on his head. This protuberance is thought to be an indication of increased brainpower. As Austin told Erik Davis in an article on Buddhism and neuroscience, "I read it [the topknot] as a metaphor for an expansion of faculties. But these new capacities are no more magical than the fact that the brains of *Homo sapiens* are larger, more convoluted and efficient than the brains of Neanderthals. Biological brain evolution is a fact, and I hope that in another 200,000 years there will be a *Homo sapiens sapiens.*"[28]

The Ageless Wisdom tells us that our spiritual perception grows "slowly and surely, as the brain becomes capable of illumination from the soul."[29] Over time, as the brain becomes more and more receptive to subtle information, our conscious awareness of the spiritual world grows.

The last book Gopi Krishna wrote before his death in 1984 was *The Way to Self-Knowledge*, a short book of verse. This book, which Krishna said was dictated from the "Super-Mind" over a period of just two weeks, contains several verses on the brain:

> About the nature of the soul . . .
> This is beyond the normal brain,
> Which needs a rare organic change
> . . . to bring the intangible plane
> Of the soul within its widened range.
> No expert study of the brain
> Can yield . . . the slightest clue
> To help empiricists to gain
> The knowledge of its nature true.
> They ne'er can pick up any trace
> Of this discarnate spark divine,
> If all the experts join the race
> In one, a mile wide, endless line.
> Vibrations from the realm sublime,
> Beyond the reach of intellect,
> Empiricists in any clime
> Cannot observe, record, detect.
> And that is why the human mind
> Is tinged with religious awe,
> With Hope and Faith, at times e'en blind,
> To honor this supernal Law.[30]

In the next chapter, I will describe the three types of telepathy and show you how we use our minds and emotions to send and receive telepathic information. I will also show you how the experience we call genius occurs when the brain registers the light of the soul.

Chapter Four

THE THREE TYPES OF TELEPATHY

There is a voice that doesn't use words. Listen.

—Rumi

In experiments dating back to the nineteenth century, scientists have validated two types of telepathy: instinctual, or feeling-based, telepathy and mental, or mind-to-mind, telepathy. According to the Wisdom teachings, there is also another, higher type of telepathy called soul-to-soul, or spiritual, telepathy.

As we saw in chapter 1, our etheric bodies are part of an interactive sea of energy that connects us to everyone and everything in our world. It is through our etheric bodies that we both send and receive telepathic information. In chapter 2, I explained how our energy centers relate to different levels of telepathic perception. In this chapter, I will describe each type of telepathy in detail and show you just how universal these teachings are. I will also show you how our pioneering scientists are, once again, validating this ancient wisdom.

INSTINCTUAL TELEPATHY

Instinctual telepathy is the lowest type of telepathy. We share this type of telepathy with the animal kingdom, and it is still a common mode of communication in indigenous cultures. Instinctual telepathy utilizes the area around the solar plexus, the center of instinct and emotion. In this type of telepathy, one person registers the feelings or needs of another at a distance. As you will see below, this teaching can be found in a wide variety of cultures, both ancient and modern. In every culture, the area around the solar plexus is key.

The kahunas, the native priests of Hawaii, believe that telepathic messages are sent directly from one solar plexus to another. According to the kahunas, the *aka*, or etheric body, of one person sends out a "finger" or thread of aka substance to the solar plexus of another. This sticky substance connects the two like a "silver spider web." Telepathic messages are sent out along these threads. After the instinctive, or "low," self receives the message, it relays the information to the rational, or "middle," self, where it "rises in the mind" like a memory. When repeated contact is made, these threads eventually become braided into an aka "cord," which creates a strong telepathic bond between two people. Aka threads can be sent to strangers by means of a glance or a handshake.[1]

The African Bushmen communicate in a similar way. As anthropologist Bradford Keeney discovered, the Bushmen of the Kalahari Desert believe that all living creatures are connected by a silver stream of energy that extends from one belly button to another. The Bushmen use these horizontal "lines" like telephone wires to send and receive telepathic messages.[2]

The Australian aboriginals believe it is their *miwi* that makes it possible for them to see or hear at a distance. *Miwi*, a Ngarrindjeri word that translates as "soul" or "instinct," is located in the pit of the stomach. Passed from parent to child, the miwi is present in everyone; but it is particularly strong in their medicine men, who use it to cast out illness and visit the spirits of the dead. A strong miwi also makes it possible to see visions and predict future events.[3]

The Japanese also rely on the solar plexus area for instinctive, nonverbal information. A Japanese businessman will often use *haragei*, or "belly talk," to size up a potential partner or business proposal. The word *haragei* derives from *hara*, translated as "belly" or "guts," and *gei*, which translates as "the art of." Many older Japanese take pride in depending on "the art of the belly" when making important business decisions. A business deal will often be called off if the haragei is not harmonious. In Japan, young businessmen are told that "in their twenties, they must improve their minds, but in their thirties they must develop their hara."[4]

In our culture, the term *gut feeling* is the most common way to explain our instinctive feelings about a person or situation. We say, "I trusted my gut in making that decision" or, "My gut told me not to trust this or that person." This term has long been used in the business and law-enforcement communities. Businessmen use the term *gut hunch* to describe their instinctive reactions to an idea or proposal, while police detectives refer to their "blue sense" as a way to describe their gut feelings about a crime.

In 2004, parapsychologists Dean Radin and Marilyn Schlitz conducted an experiment at the Institute of Noetic Sciences with twenty-six couples to determine if the gut response of one person could be felt by another. One person, designated as the sender, was shown a series of images designed to evoke "positive, negative, calming, or neutral emotions." In another room, the reaction of the receiver was monitored by electrodes placed on the heart, skin, and stomach muscles. The experimenters found that the stronger emotions—both positive and negative—did produce measurable responses in the receiver and concluded that the gut has a "belly brain" with a "perception intelligence" of its own.[5]

The existence of a belly brain has also been backed up by medical research. It was first documented by the nineteenth-century German neurologist Leopold Auerbach and later rediscovered by

Dr. Michael Gershon, a professor at Columbia University who wrote a book in the 1990s called *The Second Brain*. This second brain is made up of billions of nerve cells in the digestive tract. Some medical researchers now believe that the belly brain may be the source of the unconscious gut reactions that are later communicated to the main brain.[6]

Biologist Rupert Sheldrake, the author of two books on this subject, has done more than anyone to validate this type of telepathy scientifically. In *The Sense of Being Stared At and Other Aspects of the Extended Mind*, he summarizes his research on this subject. He also believes this type of telepathic communication to be instinctual, calling it part of our "evolutionary heritage, an aspect of our biological, animal nature."[7]

Sheldrake and his associates have collected over five thousand case histories illustrating this type of telepathy. An additional twenty thousand people have participated in a variety of experimental tests—the most recent involving text and e-mail messages. While largely unconscious, this type of telepathic perception still plays an important role in modern life. Because it utilizes the center of emotion, instinctual telepathy depends on strong emotional bonds between two people. The most common examples are between parents and children, husbands and wives, lovers, and best friends. According to Sheldrake, the most striking examples of instinctive telepathy involve intense emotion—emergencies, death, or distress.[8]

In *Ropes to God: Experiencing the Bushman Spiritual Universe*, Keeney includes a Bushman's description of this type of telepathy:

> You cannot send a thought to another person without first being filled with heightened emotion. . . . In this state you mix your thought, message or directive with your intensified feeling and

make the thought a pure feeling. It is concentrated in your belly where the intensity of your feeling escalates to a point where it can no longer be held. Then it is released along the line coming out of your belly and directed to another person's belly. They immediately respond when you communicate in this way. It may seem like we send our thoughts, but we are actually sending our feelings. Not weak, arbitrary feelings, but intense, almost overwhelming feelings. . . . A thought, message or request is changed into a feeling. . . . The feeling is the carrier.[9]

In the late 1960s, Marcia Emery was driving in downtown Washington, DC, when her brakes suddenly failed. According to Marcia,

When I put my foot on the brake, it went right to the floor. The emergency brake didn't work either. I had the choice of either crashing into the cars on the street or running into people on the sidewalk. I suddenly heard an inner voice say, "Make a quick right." I turned into an alley and smashed into a wall between two men's clothing stores, narrowly missing a pedestrian.

I survived with only scratches on my elbows and knees. My car was completely totaled—it crumpled like an accordion. On my way home, I decided not to tell my mother about the accident. I was planning to drive to Philadelphia to visit her in a few weeks and I didn't want her to worry.

I was still shaking when I got home. As I walked through the door, the telephone rang. It was my mother and her first words were "How's your car?" When I asked her how she knew, she said, "I don't know; the words just came out of my mouth."[10]

Sheldrake also collected stories of people who instantly knew that a loved one had died. While researching this chapter, I discovered that several of my friends have had this experience. One friend shared this story with me:

> My mother died from endometrial cancer. When I got the call that the end was near, I flew from California to Wisconsin to say goodbye. I took a "red-eye" flight and fell asleep on the plane. When I woke up, tears were running down my cheeks and I knew, in that moment, that my mother had just died. When I got to Chicago to change planes, my brother was waiting at the airport. Before he could speak, I said, "I already know mom died." I later saw that her death certificate recorded the exact time I woke up on that plane.

This kind of telepathy also operates in a more benign way with the people we are closest to. I had a birthday while working on this chapter. A few days before, while driving home from the library I was thinking about my interest in esoteric Christianity when the thought suddenly popped into my mind that I'd like to have a cross necklace. I thought of my one-year baby picture and the tiny gold cross I wore around my neck, a gift from my favorite uncle. A few days later, a cross necklace arrived in the mail—a birthday present from my sister. When I called to thank her, she said, "I don't know why, but as soon as I saw that necklace, I just had to get it for you."

Animal Telepathy

Instinctive telepathy is easy to spot in animals. Mass telepathy, the lowest form of instinctual telepathy, is seen in the mysterious migration patterns of birds, fish, insects, and other animals. Sheldrake points out that the English swallow travels six thousand miles to its winter feeding grounds in Africa in the fall. After spending the winter in its breeding grounds in Baja California, Mexico, the grey whale swims four thousand miles to the Bering Sea. Monarch butterflies, born near the Great Lakes, fly two thousand miles to the Mexican highlands for the winter. Scientists have theories but no clear answers as to how animals manage to navigate these vast distances year after year.

Instinctive telepathy between animals and humans is also apparent. Once again, this contact is dependent upon close relationships. Sheldrake explored this type of telepathy in his book *Dogs That Know When Their Owners Are Coming Home and Other Unexplained Powers of Animals*. In this book, Sheldrake provides the results of his research on the perceptiveness of dogs, cats, parrots, horses, and other animals. His research included random surveys of more than a thousand pet owners and interviews with hundreds of people who work with animals, such as dog handlers, veterinarians, kennel and stable proprietors, horse trainers and riders. He discovered that dogs and other animals often anticipate their owners' arrival, even when the owners return home at random times or in unfamiliar vehicles.

Sheldrake carried out an extensive videotaped experiment with Jaytee, a mixed-breed terrier owned by Pamela Smart, his research assistant. When Pam went out, she often left Jaytee with her parents, who lived in the flat next door. The experiment started with both Pam and her parents keeping a log of her travels and Jaytee's reaction to her return. According to Sheldrake, Jaytee anticipated her return by waiting at the window ten or more minutes in eighty-five of one hundred occasions, even when she returned at different times and by unusual means—a bicycle, train, or taxi.[11]

Sheldrake also recorded many other examples of human-to-animal telepathy, including dogs who knew when their owners were thinking about going for a walk, and cats who knew in advance when they were to be taken to the vet. He also recorded stories of cats, dogs, and even horses who found their way back home from a great distance.

As a child, I was fascinated by my father's tales of his childhood pet, a fox terrier named Whitey. Whitey spent his days lying in the sun on the back porch of my grandparents' home in Yreka, a small town in Northern California. At a certain time each weekday afternoon, Whitey would scratch at the back door until my grandmother let him out. He would then trot through the streets until he arrived at my father's elementary school, a mile away. Whitey was always waiting, wagging his tail in greeting, when my father walked out of school at 3:00 pm. How did he know what time to leave, I wondered? How did he find his way?

Perhaps like Jaytee, Whitey was responding to my father's anticipation of the final school bell. His ability to find his way to the school each day may have been a function of the "morphic field" that links owners with their beloved pets.

Mental Telepathy

Mental telepathy, or thought transference, is mind-to-mind telepathy. This type of telepathy utilizes the throat center and the lower levels of the mental plane. The practice of true mental telepathy requires a concentrated, one-pointed focus of attention. Unlike trance channeling—a type of mediumship in which a disembodied entity uses a channel's body to communicate a message—telepathic contact is made between two fully conscious, focused minds. Three examples of this type of telepathic communication can be found in the work of Helena Blavatsky, Helena Roerich, and Alice Bailey.

In the past two centuries, the books of Blavatsky, Roerich, and Bailey have introduced the Ageless Wisdom teachings to the general public. Each of these women was said to have functioned as an *amanuensis*, or "one who takes dictation," for a group of Tibetan masters living in the Himalayas. Helena Blavatsky, founder of the Theosophical Society, was thought to have been an advanced initiate of the mystery teachings. Her books include *Isis Unveiled*, published in 1877, and *The Secret Doctrine: The Synthesis of Science, Religion, and Philosophy*, published in 1888. *The Secret Doctrine*, a two-volume set on the evolution of man and the cosmos, influenced both esotericists and scientists. One admirer was Albert Einstein, who reportedly kept a copy of *The Secret Doctrine* on his desk.[12]

Helena Roerich, cofounder of the Agni Yoga Society, began her work with the masters in 1920. Her telepathic contact with the Tibetan master Morya produced a series of sixteen books on a spiritual philosophy she called "living ethics."[13]

Alice Bailey's work with the Tibetan master Djwal Khul began in 1919. At fifteen, she received a surprise visit from a turbaned man who told her he would have work for her to do in the future. Twenty-four years later, then a mother of three, she suddenly heard a "voice" within asking for her cooperation in the writing of a series of books. After some reluctance, she agreed. According to Bailey, in the beginning she simply listened and wrote down the dictated words as they were "dropped into my brain, one by one."[14] Over time, as their minds became attuned, she was able to directly register and write down the thoughts and ideas of the Tibetan master. Over a thirty-year period, they produced a total of nineteen books on consciousness and evolution. It was Bailey who introduced the term *new age* into the popular culture.

Another example of mind-to-mind telepathy is the direct transmission practiced by the Buddhist teacher Padmasambhava, who brought Buddhist practices from India to Tibet in the eighth century. Padmasambhava was said to have concealed teachings, texts, and religious objects to be discovered by later generations. The teachings, called *termas*, or "spiritual treasures," are transmitted mentally to masters called *tertons*, or "treasure finders," in two ways.

The earth termas are symbolic texts written on yellow scrolls. These scrolls are concealed in rocks, lakes, and temples. Once found, these symbols would reawaken the terton's conscious mind to the guru's teachings. Mind termas are direct mind-to-mind transmissions from guru to terton. These teachings are concealed within the terton's mind in the form of letters or sounds. At the appropriate time, the terton becomes consciously aware of the transmitted information. These forms of direct transmission have allowed the teachings to be passed down from one generation to the next in an unbroken lineage.[15] True mental telepathy is still fairly rare. According to Bailey, mind-to-mind telepathy will be the preferred mode of communication in about four hundred years. More common today is the type of mental telepathy that occurs on the astral levels, as described in chapter 1. Scientific experiments on this type of mental telepathy date back to the 1880s. According to Dean Radin, the first study of mental telepathy was done by a British physicist named Sir William Barrett in 1883. In his first book, *The Conscious Universe*, Radin traced the history of telepathic research and described the best-known experiments: Upton Sinclair's experiments with his wife, Mary Craig Kimbrough; the ESP card tests carried out at Duke University; the dream telepathy experiments conducted at Maimonides Institute in Brooklyn, New York; and the ganzfeld telepathy experiments conducted in the mid-1970s. I've included a brief overview of these experiments below.

Mental Radio

Pulitzer Prize–winning author Upton Sinclair was best known for his novel *The Jungle*, a book that exposed the unsanitary conditions in the meatpacking industry and led to the passage of the Meat Inspection Act in 1906.

In the late 1920s, Sinclair conducted a series of three hundred telepathy experiments with his wife, Mary Craig Kimbrough. Sinclair would create an image and place it in a sealed envelope. In another room, Mary Craig would "tune in" to the image and attempt to draw a duplicate copy. In 1930, Sinclair published a book called *Mental Radio*, which described these experiments. Mary Craig's accuracy rate was impressive enough to attract the attention of several high-profile friends. One such friend was Albert Einstein, who wrote the preface to the book, praising Sinclair for his conscientious reporting. The book also attracted the attention of William McDougall, a former psychology professor at Oxford and Harvard, who was then considered the "dean of American psychology." McDougall was so impressed with Mary Craig's abilities that he created a parapsychology department at Duke University to study paranormal activity.

ESP Card Tests

While at Duke University, J. B. Rhine, McDougall's assistant and eventual successor, devised telepathy experiments with a series of cards. The cards, designed by Karl Zerner, a colleague of Rhine's, were called the Zerner ESP cards. The cards consisted of five symbols: a circle, a cross, a square, a star, and an image consisting of three wavy, vertical lines. A deck consisted of five cards of each symbol. In this experiment, the sender would shuffle the cards, and as each card was turned over, he or she would attempt to send the image mentally to the receiver in another room.

Dream Telepathy Experiments

The first dream telepathy experiments were done by the Italian researcher G. B. Ermacora in the 1880s. More controlled experiments were done in the 1960s and early 1970s by a team of parapsychologists at the Maimonides Institute in Brooklyn, New York. These experiments included a receiver and a sender. The receiver would spend the night in a soundproof, electronically shielded dream lab. Once the receiver fell asleep, she would be monitored for the rapid eye movements that indicate the dream state. The sender would then try to mentally transmit a randomly chosen image to the dreamer. Once this was done, the receiver was awakened and asked to describe her dream. This process would be repeated several times during the night. The information from the dreamer was recorded, transcribed, and later compared with the sender's image.

Ganzfeld Telepathy Experiments

Ganzfeld, German for "whole field," is a type of experiment that attempts to mimic the state of deep meditation when our physical senses are stilled and no longer relaying information about the physical world to our brains. In this experiment, the receiver and sender are placed in separate, insulated cubicles. The receiver's eyes are covered with halves of Ping-Pong balls and his ears are covered with headphones playing white noise. Once the receiver is relaxed, the sender is shown still photos or film clips. The sender then attempts to telepathically send these images to the receiver. The receiver's impressions are recorded and compared with the original image.

According to Radin, the results from each of the experiments discussed above—ESP, dream telepathy, and ganzfeld—were "statistically significant" and provided clear scientific evidence that this type of mental telepathy does exist.[16]

SPIRITUAL TELEPATHY

Spiritual, or soul-to-soul, telepathy is the highest type of telepathy. This type of telepathy utilizes the higher levels of the mental plane. Spiritual telepathy becomes possible only when we've created a link between the brain, mind, and soul.

When we align the brain, mind, and soul, we have the ability to serve as intermediaries between the physical and the spiritual worlds. The Masters who guide the evolution of our planet cannot directly affect life on earth. Instead, they look for those with a direct line of communication between the soul and the brain. Information and ideas can then be stepped down via the soul and "impressed" upon our brains. Once the information is anchored on earth, it is dispersed into thought currents that register on the general public. The flood of intuition books in the 1990s and the current interest in the higher functions of the mind are good examples of many minds registering the same impulse at the same time.

At times, ideas are also given to specific individuals. According to Bailey, thoughts about a project or action can be "thrown down into our brains."[17] She uses the birth of the League of Nations, the forerunner of the United Nations, as an example. According to Bailey, the idea of an international organization devoted to world peace was stepped down from the higher planes until it registered in the brain of Colonel Edward House, an advisor and confidant to Woodrow Wilson. House and President

Wilson were so close that Wilson once declared, "Mr. House is my second personality. . . . His thoughts and mine are one." Wilson, who is often mistakenly credited with the idea, asked House to draft the constitution for the League in 1918.[18]

The story I described in the introduction, in which I suddenly registered a thought I knew was not my own, is another example of this experience. Sim Simran, the publisher of *11:11 Magazine*, had a similar one. Sim explained:

> In 2007, my life was falling apart and I was deeply depressed. I was going through a painful separation and had just ended a thirty-year career in my family's business. I had lost everything—my identity, my marriage, the support of my family. During this time, I started seeing the numbers 11:11 everywhere—on clocks, license plates, and mailboxes—it happened so frequently I was starting to think I was losing my mind.
>
> One night, during the darkest period of my depression, I woke up, looked at the clock—which amazingly, had just turned 11:11—and immediately saw a series of images as they flashed through my mind. I saw the numbers 11:11 on a series of magazine covers, an internet radio show banner and as a television logo. In that moment, I mentally "heard" the words, "Do this now. You will heal; others will heal."
>
> I had always known that 11:11 was a "master number" associated with the soul and, through additional research, I discovered more of its symbolism. I followed the direction I received and now, *11:11: A Magazine Devoted to the Journey of the Soul* is distributed around the world. 11:11 Talk Radio reaches almost 300,000 people each week and my TV program will launch soon. My goal is to help others move through their pain and discover their soul's true purpose.[19]

When we learn to access higher levels of information, we become as "the arms and legs" of God. We have the ability to bring to earth the divine ideas and enlightened solutions we need to solve the most pressing problems of our time. We can use the information we receive to help humanity in many ways—as educators, humanitarians, healers, writers, artists, and entrepreneurs.

Our most celebrated creative thinkers—those people we call geniuses or visionaries—have all had the ability to access the subtle world of the soul. We see the fruits of this experience all around us, from our most beautiful works of art to the scientific breakthroughs and inventions that have revolutionized our world. Many of our most renowned artists, writers, scientists, and business leaders have left a record of this experience.

In the late 1800s, Arthur Abell, an American violinist living in Europe, interviewed Puccini, Brahms, Strauss, Wagner, and other well-known composers about the source of their creative genius. As you'll see below, their experiences are remarkably consistent. Each spoke of the soul as the portal to a universal source of inspiration. Once they were connected to this source, ideas and images simply flowed into their brains.

As Puccini explained to Abell, "The great secret of all creative geniuses is that they possess the power to appropriate the beauty, the wealth, the grandeur, and the sublimity within their own souls, which are a part of the Omnipotence, and to communicate those riches to others. The conscious, purposeful appropriation of one's own soul force is the supreme secret." Puccini experienced inspiration as a divine force, a "vibration [that passes] from the soul-center, into my consciousness, where the inspired ideas are born."[20]

German composer Richard Wagner, best known for his set of four operas called the *Ring*, also spoke of inspiration as the ability to become one with the "universal currents of Divine thought [that are] vibrating everywhere." According to Wagner, "This universal vibrating energy binds the soul of man . . . to the Supreme Force of the universe, of which we are all a part." Wagner, who also spoke of "appropriating" this force when composing his famous operas, described his creative process to Abell: "I see in my mind's eye definite visions of the heroes and heroines of my music dramas. I have clear mental pictures of them before they take form in my scores, and while I am holding fast to those mental images, the music . . . the whole musical structure, occurs to me."[21]

Richard Strauss also spoke of inspiration as coming from a higher self: "In my most inspired moods, I have definite compelling visions, involving a higher selfhood. I feel at such moments that I am tapping the source of infinite and eternal energy from which you and I and all things proceed." Strauss, who called his ability to register inspired ideas a "divine gift," described a similar experience while writing one of his operas: "The ideas were flowing in upon me—the motives, themes, structure, melodies . . . in fact the entire musical measure by measure. . . . I was definitely conscious of being aided by a more than earthly power."[22]

Johannes Brahms called his method of composing music "communicating with the infinite." Composing, Brahms said, "cannot be done by will power working through the conscious mind. . . . It can only be accomplished by the soul-powers within." He described inspiration as "a condition where the conscious mind is in temporary abeyance and the superconscious is in control, for it is through the superconscious mind, which is part of Omnipotence, that the inspiration comes."[23] As Brahms explained:

I . . . feel vibrations which thrill my whole being. . . . In this exalted state I see clearly what is obscure in my ordinary moods; I then feel capable of drawing inspiration from above as Beethoven did. . . .

Those vibrations assume the form of distinct mental images. . . . The ideas flow in upon me, directly from God, and not only do I see distinct themes in my mind's eye, but they are clothed in the right forms, harmonies and orchestration. Measure by measure the finished project is revealed to me."[24]

Writers and visual artists have also reported this experience. As Ralph Waldo Emerson explained in his 1844 essay *The Poet*, "It is a secret which every intellectual man quickly learns, that beyond the energy of his possessed and conscious intellect, he is capable of a new energy . . . a great public power on which he can draw . . . by unlocking his human doors . . . he is caught up in the life of the Universe."[25] Beat poet Alan Ginsberg had this experience while reading the mystical poetry of William Blake. As Ginsberg told one biographer,

I had the impression of the entire universe . . . filled with light and intelligence and communication. . . . Kind of like the top of my head coming off, letting the rest of the universe into my own brain. . . . There was a sense of an Eternal Father completely conscious . . . in whom I had just awakened. I had just awakened into his brain, or into his consciousness, a larger consciousness than my own. . . . [It was] the consciousness of the entire universe."[26]

Leonardo da Vinci and Michelangelo, two of our most renowned artists, also spoke of this experience. As da Vinci put it, "The painter's mind is a copy of the Divine Mind," and "the painter has the Universe in his mind and hands. . . . Where the spirit does not work with the hand, there is no art."[27] Michelangelo also believed his creative inspiration came from a higher source. As he wrote, "Every beauty which is seen here below . . . resembles more than anything else that celestial source from which we all come."[28] He was said to have embedded this message on one of the panels he painted on the ceiling of the Sistine Chapel. In this image—later titled *The Creation of Adam*— God extends his hand to a reclining man. The vehicle carrying God to Adam is an exact replica of the human brain with a spinal cord, brain stem, and pituitary gland—the brain being key to our conscious awareness of the subtle worlds.

Akiane Kramarik is one modern-day example. Raised in a non-religious home in the Midwest, Akiane was only four when she surprised her mother by describing a series of intense spiritual experiences. According to Akiane, God had shown her a vision of heaven, a place of unearthly beauty where flowers were the color and transparency of precious stones and plants could think, move, and sing.

Soon after, she developed an intense urge to draw. She began with pencil drawings at four, moved on to pastels at six, and began painting with oils soon after. Her paintings, which now range in price from fifty thousand to one million dollars, include images of Jesus, angels, and other spiritual themes. Before she begins a new painting, Akiane goes out into nature to pray and ask for ideas. The words and images then appear inside her head. Akiane, who donates a significant portion of each sale to charity, believes God works through her as she paints. The purpose of her art, she says, is to transmit spiritual messages to the world and to bring people closer to God.[29]

I also found an example of this experience in the business world. Konosuke Matsushita, the founder of Matsushita, one of the world's largest manufacturers of consumer electronic products, believed his extraordinary success was due to his ability to access *kongen*, a Japanese term meaning the "the root or origin of universal energy." Matsushita, whose company brand names include National and Panasonic, encouraged his top executives to tune into the wisdom of the universal mind by making meditation part of their daily work routine.[30]

SCIENCE AND RELIGION

Isaac Newton and Albert Einstein, two of our greatest scientists, also left records of this experience. Isaac Newton, author of the *Principia*, one of the most important scientific books ever written, invented calculus and formulated the three laws of motion that form the basis of classical mechanics.

The man many call "the father of modern science" was also a serious occultist who studied alchemy, numerology, astrology, and biblical prophecy. Many believe his study of alchemy was key to his scientific breakthroughs. Newton's method of discovery was to hold a problem in his mind "for hours, days, or weeks" until the answer was revealed. As Newton himself put it, "I keep the subject of my inquiry constantly before me, and wait till the first dawning opens gradually, little by little, into a full and clear light."[31]

Einstein's theory of relativity transformed theoretical physics. His famous equation $E = mc^2$ came in a moment of inspiration when, in his words, "a storm broke loose in my mind and with it came the answers." Einstein, a friend later said, had "tapped into God's thoughts and tuned into the master plan for the universe." After his death, pathologists dissected and probed Einstein's brain, looking for anomalies that would explain the source of his genius. But Einstein—who wrote, "There comes a time when the mind takes a higher plane of knowledge. . . . All great discoveries have involved such a leap" and "The mystical . . . is the source of all true art and science"—made it clear that his inspiration came from a higher source.[32]

The experience of spiritual telepathy has also changed the course of history. Joan of Arc was a peasant girl who lived in the village of Domremy, in the Champagne district of northeastern France. In 1426, at the age of fourteen, she heard divine "voices" telling her that it was her mission to save her homeland from English domination. Five years later, she persuaded a local baron to send her to the castle of Charles of Ponthieu, heir to the French throne, where she announced, "I am sent here by God, the King of Heaven."[33] After gaining the approval of the Church council, she was allowed to lead Charles's army. After several swift victories, the English were driven to the north of France and Charles was crowned King in the cathedral of Reims.

Illumination, a state of pure intuitive perception, is the highest type of spiritual telepathy. It was this experience that produced our religious scriptures. According to Hindu tradition, the Vedas, the sacred scriptures of India, are *apaurueya*, or "not human compositions." The Hindus believe these scriptures were given by God to their ancient seers through direct intuitive revelation. These seers were called the *mantra-drashta*, or "seers of thought." The texts are collectively called *Shruti*, a Sanskrit word meaning "heard" or "revealed."

In a Buddhist text on the four noble truths, the Buddha declared that this teaching was "not among doctrines handed down" but that "there arose within him the eye to perceive them, the knowledge of their nature and the understanding of their cause."[34]

Moses received a divine revelation to lead the enslaved Israelites out of Egypt to the Promised Land. According to Jewish tradition, the content of the Torah was later revealed to him by God on Mount Sinai. As Moses came down from the mount, tablets in hand, "the skin of his face shone and all the sons of Israel were afraid to come near him" (Ex. 34:30).

The Muslims consider Mohammed to be the final prophet and messenger of God. While meditating in the cave of Hira near Mecca in the year 610, Mohammed reportedly received his first revelation from God, through the angel Gabriel. The revelations continued, and, over the next twenty-three years, Mohammed's followers recorded the text of what later became Islam's holy book, the Koran.

Accessing the Soul

As you'll see in the coming chapters, it's not just the "special" people—our famous artists, scientists, business and religious leaders—who have the ability to contact the subtle worlds. It is possible for each of us to build our bridge to the soul and tap that universal flow of wisdom and knowledge. Accessing the subtle worlds is a step-by-step process that begins with the refinement of our physical, emotional, and mental bodies. When we purify the physical body and learn to calm our minds and emotions, we create an unimpeded channel for the free flow of information from the soul to the brain. Physical ailments, fatigue, and mental or emotional static will deflect the subtle currents of thought emanating from the higher planes, making it hard for our brains to register higher wisdom and ideas. In the next chapter, I will introduce you to refinement practices from a variety of spiritual traditions. I will share my own experiences and introduce you to other people who have also used these practices.

Chapter Five

REFINING YOUR PHYSICAL, EMOTIONAL, AND MENTAL BODIES

Watch your thoughts, for they become words.
Watch your words, for they become actions.
Watch your actions, for they become habits.
Watch your habits, for they become character.
Watch your character, for it becomes your destiny.

—Lao Tzu

The first step in esoteric training is the refinement of our physical, emotional, and mental bodies. Refinement is a process of eliminating bad habits, cultivating virtues, and removing the blocks that limit our access to the higher worlds. Refinement practices can be found in all our spiritual traditions. These teachings vary from the noble eightfold path of the Buddha, to the development of the Christian virtues, to the teachings on character refinement found in Judaism and Islam. Although the methods vary from tradition to tradition, the requirements and goals are the same: purity of body, control of the emotions, and stability of mind.

When we refine our physical, emotional, and mental bodies, we become esoteric "engineers." Unlike electrical engineers, who create satellite dishes and other hardware, we turn our bodies into sensitive instruments capable of receiving and interpreting a wide range of frequencies. Think of a radio receiver: when we want to tune in to our favorite station, we adjust our receiver to that particular frequency. When we refine our bodies, we are adjusting our frequency to more easily "tune in" to the subtle vibrations of the higher planes.

We build bodies that resonate with the energy of the higher worlds by eating pure foods and getting adequate rest and exercise. During the refinement stage, all spiritual traditions stress the need for a healthy diet and regular habits of sleeping and eating. This teaching is illustrated in a verse from the Bhagavad Gita: "There is no meditation for the man who eats too little or for the man who eats too much, or for him whose habit it is to sleep too much or too little. But for him who is regulated in food, in work; regulated also in sleep and in waking, meditation becomes the destroyer of all suffering."[1]

Dietary recommendations can be found in all our spiritual traditions. The Buddhists and Hindus both believe that food affects not only the body but the mind and spirit as well. For the Hindus, a proper diet is essential to spiritual development. Their scriptures state, "When food is pure, the mind is pure."[2] They divide food into three categories: *tamasic, rajasic,* and *sattvic.* They believe that tamasic food—processed, overripe, or spoiled food—promotes anger, greed, and other negative emotions. Rajasic foods—meat, as well as salty or spicy foods—promote passions and a restless mind. Sattvic foods—fruits, vegetables, nuts, and whole grains—promote mental clarity and a calm spirit.

Buddhists are taught to eat mindfully by a practice called the "five contemplations while eating." In this exercise, Buddhists ask themselves a series of questions about the nature, origin, and timing of each meal. Buddhists are also taught to avoid meat, intoxicants, and the "five pungent spices"—onions, garlic, leeks, scallions, and chives—thought to have a detrimental effect on our internal organs. Dietary recommendations and requirements can also be found in the Bible and the Qur'an.

As we saw in chapter 3, the downpouring of subtle energy from the soul physically alters the brain. Over time, this energy will alter every cell in our bodies. As LaUna Huffines, author of several books on the Wisdom teachings, explains, "We are bringing a finer submolecular substance to our bodies. This substance builds higher quality cells that create a resonance between our bodies and the higher energies. These cells thrive and grow on pure, fresh food."[3]

I spoke with several long-time students of the Ageless Wisdom about their methods of refining the physical body. Every person told me that natural, unprocessed foods and pure water were absolutely essential. Losing the taste for meat is common, and many of the people I spoke with gradually adopted a vegetarian diet. Others felt that their bodies still needed animal protein. Many of those I spoke with followed the diets prescribed in *Eat Right 4 Your Type*, which recommends specific foods for each blood type.[4]

I am not a strict vegetarian, but over time, the act of chewing flesh—even fish—has become repulsive to me, and I have gradually adopted a mostly vegetarian diet. Marsha Mason, a massage therapist from Chicago, has had a similar experience. As she explained to me,

After I was introduced to the Wisdom teachings, I began to meditate twice daily, at sunrise and sunset. I wasn't trying to become a vegetarian, but I gradually lost my taste for certain kinds of protein. Eggs were the first to go, and soon after, I lost my taste for chicken and red meat. It was effortless; I began to feel lighter, and I found it easier to meditate. I could go into the stillness and more easily access information from above. My intuition became sharper, and my healing abilities were also heightened. I could put my hands on someone and instantly pick up the energy blocks in their bodies.[5]

Steven Lumiere told me that garlic interferes with his ability to meditate deeply and access telepathic information. According to Lumiere, garlic shuts down theta brain waves and desynchronizes the left and right hemispheres of our brains. He also avoids onions, chives, and other stimulating foods.[6]

There is no one-size-fits-all when it comes to diet, and, as your body absorbs and integrates the higher frequencies, you will be prompted to eat the foods your body needs. Eat intuitively: pay attention to your body's likes and dislikes, and experiment with tastes, flavors, textures, and amounts.

According to the Wisdom teachings, a diet centered on fresh, organic fruits and vegetables, nuts, seeds, grains, and pure water will make our bodies "fit vehicles for the soul."[7] LaUna Huffines recommends choosing fruits and vegetables by color. As Huffines writes, "Green foods vibrate with a purifying energy, which helps us to excrete toxins. Orange fruits and vegetables will build a very fine cellular structure. Golden fruits and vegetables supplement the spiritual vibrations flowing into our eyes and head."[8] Gabriel Cousens, author of *Spiritual Nutrition*, also recommends choosing our food by color. According to Cousens, the color of our food is a key to its energy pattern and the effect it will have on the cells and tissues in our bodies. Intuitively choosing foods by color will help us to provide our bodies with the specific nutrients we need. Both Huffines and Cousens stress the need to include raw foods, which maintain their "living essence." According to Cousens, this diet, rich in sattvic foods, will expand our minds and turn our bodies into "superconductors of the Divine."[9]

As your body starts to integrate the subtle energies, you may become hypersensitive to certain foods. When I first began to experiment with these practices, I developed a splitting headache if I ate sugar, wheat, or dairy foods. I eliminated sugar from my diet, but as my body became more accustomed to the influx of subtle energies, I was able to eat wheat and dairy foods without ill effects. Many of the people I spoke with also developed sensitivity to sugar and reported feeling bloated, depressed, or fatigued after eating sweets. Increased sensitivity to alcohol was also common.

The way food is grown is also important. Food grown with respect for the earth has a higher vibration than commercial crops grown in depleted soil. Many years before the local food movement, Edgar Cayce—the most famous psychic of the twentieth century—indicated that locally grown, seasonal foods contained the highest and most harmonious vibration for our bodies.[10]

Food prepared with love has the highest vibration of all.[11] Before Cousens prepares a meal, he goes to his garden and intuitively chooses the vegetables he feels his body needs. He thanks the individual plants for feeding him and prepares his meal with love and gratitude for the gifts of nature. Saying grace before each meal, a practice found in many cultures and spiritual traditions, is another way to raise the vibration of the food we eat.

It is important to take your health into consideration before experimenting with the meditations in this book. An illness will make it difficult—even dangerous—to integrate the higher, faster vibrations of the subtle planes. If you have an illness, make regaining your health your first priority. When I first started exploring this subject, I was depleted from years of deadline pressure and made the decision to focus on my health before experimenting with these practices. Projecting our attention upward takes mental strength and stamina. I've noticed that when I am tired, it is difficult to sustain these practices. The need to protect our health is illustrated in two quotes from an ancient kabbalistic text included in

Spiritual Nutrition: "When the body ails, the soul too is weakened," and "The welfare of the soul can only be achieved after obtaining the welfare of the body."[12]

Another way to raise the vibration of the physical body is through the ancient arts of Tai Chi and Qigong. The slow, precise movements used in these practices stimulate the flow of subtle energy, or chi, within our bodies. Cultivating our chi makes it easier to harmonize our personal energy with the subtle energy of the universe.

Over many lifetimes, our bodies become lighter and lighter as we absorb the higher vibrations of the subtle planes and discard the heavier atoms that keep us anchored to the earth. The ability to levitate like Indian yogis can occur when our bodies contain the necessary percentage of lighter atoms.

THE EMOTIONAL BODY

From the earliest times, the need to quiet our emotions has been seen as an essential step on the road to spiritual development. To access higher wisdom and guidance, our emotional bodies must be still and calm. In most spiritual disciplines, the emphasis is put on quieting the mental body. When we refine our bodies, it's best to work from the bottom up. Quieting the mind becomes easier when our emotional bodies are calm.

As Jacob Needleman points out, Socrates and Plato both wrote of a universal intelligence that could awaken in man only when our emotions are mastered. The early Christians called these emotions "passions" and considered them to be a serious impediment to the pursuit of spiritual growth. Needleman has also studied the work of a fourth-century Christian named Evagrius Ponticus, who wrote of *apatheia*—Greek for "without emotions" or "freedom from emotions," the root of our word *apathy*—as the "door to contemplation." As Ponticus wrote, the practice of apatheia is an essential step in our spiritual journey, one that will eventually lead to a "deep understanding of God and the universe."[13]

Refining the emotional body is one of the biggest challenges, and the most important. Emotional turmoil will block our reception of information from the subtle planes. Our goal in purifying the emotional body is to develop a quiet spirit, a feeling of inner serenity and peace. Our emotional patterns—childhood wounds and unresolved conflicts, anger, or grief—can make inner serenity impossible to maintain.

When Jack Kornfield began to teach meditation practices, he discovered that at least half his students were unable to master the basic concentration exercises. Hindered by old wounds and unfinished business from the past, they found it impossible to sit quietly and maintain a focused point of attention. Kornfield, who spent ten years healing the trauma caused by his own painful childhood, has written extensively on the need to incorporate Western psychotherapy into contemplative spiritual practices.[14]

Most of the people I spoke to went through a similar process of confronting and clearing out old wounds and traumas. For many of us, this is a necessary first step. Letting go of our daily upsets, antagonisms, and envy of others is an ongoing process. Most of us have a trigger—some issue that creates emotional imbalance—be it anger, fear, or worry. My biggest problem is anger, and I've struggled with it a lot over the years. I've experimented with a variety of practices and found the practices below—harmlessness, forgiveness, compassion, and the nightly review, in addition to the heart-opening practices in chapter 2—to be the most helpful in calming my emotional body.

CHAPTER FIVE

Harmlessness

The practice of harmlessness is one of the best ways to gain control of our emotional bodies. This practice requires that we monitor our thoughts, words, and conduct. The practice of harmlessness includes right thought, right speech, and right action. Right speech requires that we stop all criticism, judgment, and gossip. Right thought requires that we extend goodwill to all beings. Right action requires that we act consciously, not impulsively. This practice is similar to the Eightfold Path, the practice of ethical conduct taught by the Buddha. Practicing harmlessness also prevents us from accumulating negative karma and attracts to us the same kindness and compassion we extend to others.

This discipline is harder than it seems. When I first started the practice, I was surprised how often I had negative thoughts about others. Total harmlessness is said to be possible only when we're fully aligned with our souls, but this daily practice is one of the best ways I've found to become aware of my behavior and its effect on others.

When we are harmless in thought, we curb our unkind and judgmental thoughts and instead focus our attention on positive, supportive thoughts about others. When we practice harmlessness in speech, we control our negativity, gossip, and criticism. When we practice harmlessness in action, we don't act on impulse or hurt others with our anger or depression. We refrain from dishonesty and deceitfulness and extend goodwill and kindness to all.

Tibetan Buddhism teaches that the emotional discipline of harmlessness will also redirect the energy of the lower centers to the higher. Harmlessness in thought helps to awaken the throat center, harmlessness in speech helps to awaken the heart center, and harmlessness in action helps to awaken the head center. When we are harmless, we become pure channels through which the masters of wisdom can pour their blessings out on the world. For anyone with a desire to serve, this practice is essential. The Masters of wisdom cannot work through us if we have critical tongues or separative attitudes and beliefs.

Jan Skogstrom, an interfaith minister in Minneapolis, leaves Post-it notes printed with the word *harmlessness* in various places around her house—her desk lamp, bathroom mirror, and refrigerator—as a daily reminder to watch her thoughts. As Jan explained to me, "As the Buddha said, harmful behavior begins with a thought; our thoughts become words and our words become deeds. Watching my thoughts is a daily discipline. When I notice a negative thought, I reframe it to a loving or forgiving thought instead. This helps me shift my attitude from moment to moment."[15]

Forgiveness

Harmlessness is made easier when we cultivate the virtues of forgiveness and compassion. Forgiveness has been my biggest issue and the biggest barrier I've experienced to achieving a quiet mind. And I'm not alone; when I asked the people I interviewed what they did to refine their emotional bodies, almost every person I spoke to put forgiveness at the top of his or her list. I checked out an armful of library books on forgiveness at one point and found one book especially helpful: *Forgiveness Is a Choice* by Robert Enright. In it, Enright makes an important point: true forgiveness requires that we feel compassion for the person who has hurt us.[16] Similarly, the Dalai Lama has written that "the greatest degree of inner tranquility comes from the development of compassion." He also considers it the best way to counteract negative emotions. "When you come across a chance [to practice compassion] treat it with gratitude. It is rare. Just like unexpectedly finding a treasure in your own house, you should be happy and grateful toward your enemies for providing you with that precious opportunity."[17]

When we practice forgiveness, we are not condoning another person's bad behavior; we are simply releasing its hold on us. In a perfect world, we would have a heart-to-heart talk and easily resolve any issues we have with others. Unfortunately, we don't live in a perfect world, and other people are not always able or willing to cooperate with us.

I adapted the following practices from meditations taught to me by Steven Lumiere. I use the compassion meditation daily and the forgiveness meditation as needed.

Compassion Meditation Practice

Give yourself fifteen minutes of uninterrupted quiet time. Calm yourself by closing your eyes and following your breath, in and out, for a count of ten.

1. When you are ready, think of someone you love—a mate, parent, child, or beloved friend. Feel your love for them and project compassion from your heart to their heart. Feel your heart open as you think about their lives: their challenges, difficulties, and sorrows. Repeat this process with each of your loved ones in turn. If you wish, you can also add a prayer here, from the simple "May you be free from pain and sorrow" to words that address a specific problem your loved one may have. For example, it could be "May you be free from worry," "May you be free from fear," or "May you be free from addiction."

2. When you have finished, feel and project compassion toward yourself. As you do, feel compassion for your own difficulties, struggles, and challenges. If you wish, add the prayer "May I be free from pain and sorrow," or make up your own wording.

3. Feel and project compassion toward anyone with whom you have difficulties. As you do, feel your heart open as you think about their lives, their stresses, their challenges and sorrows. Add the prayer "May you be free from pain and sorrow," or focus your prayer on a particular problem you know they have.

4. Feel and project compassion toward individuals in your town or city. Have you heard about and been moved by the suffering of someone in your community? During this step, I send compassion and prayers to people I've read about in my local newspaper or heard about on the evening news. They may not know us or consciously feel the compassion we send, but they will benefit nevertheless by the loving thoughts we send to them.

    I have a wooden box on my meditation table that I have filled with notes about the people I want to include in this meditation. My box includes notes about a woman who, overwhelmed by stress, snapped and killed her autistic son; a mentally ill woman who threw her baby off a local bridge; and a father who accidentally backed his car over his eighteen-month-old son. Create your own list and imagine that your compassionate thoughts and prayers are comforting these people and helping them to heal a little more each day.

5. Feel and project compassion toward all the people on earth. If it feels right to you, you can focus your attention on specific, hard-hit areas where people are suffering from the effects of famine, war, or natural disasters.

6. Feel and project compassion toward everything on the earth: the plants, the animals, and even the earth itself.

7. Feel and project compassion toward everything in our solar system: the sun, moon, and planets.

When you do this meditation regularly, you will notice that your heart will begin to open and compassion for others will become a habit. You'll become less judgmental and more understanding of the human frailties we all share.

Forgiveness Meditation: Standing in Their Shoes

This is one of the best forgiveness techniques I've found. When we consciously identify with the person who has angered us, when we take the time to look at life through their eyes, it is easier to understand why they act the way they do. As Steven Lumiere explained to me, "People only act according to the amount of love, will, and intelligence that has been allotted to them or cultivated in them at any one time. They are victims of these forces, and they cannot act in any other way. By temporarily identifying with them and seeing the world as they do, we gain insight into why they do what they do, which helps us forgive them and accept them as they are, since they can't be any different."[18]

1. Give yourself fifteen minutes of uninterrupted quiet time. Calm yourself by closing your eyes and following your breath, in and out, for a count of ten.

2. Imagine the person you need to forgive standing in front of you. If it is easier, you can also imagine them in their own environment— their home or office.

3. Imagine that you have stepped into their shoes and are now looking at the world through their eyes. Take a few minutes to imagine what life must be like from their perspective. Think about their past and the forces that have made them what they are today. Think about their challenges, fears, and insecurities. How would you react if you were in their shoes, with the same set of circumstances, the same limitations, the same difficulties and fears?

4. When you are ready, come back to your own body. Imagine the person you need to forgive standing in front of you, and look at them with forgiveness and compassion. Bless them, and remind yourself that, just like you, they are doing the best they can. Just like you, they have their own blind spots, wounds, and insecurities.

When I do this meditation, it's easy to see that, given the same set of circumstances, there is a good chance that I would behave exactly like the person I need to forgive.

The Nightly Review

The nightly review is an ancient spiritual practice. I have come across it in a wide variety of traditions—Tibetan Buddhism, the kabbalah, and the teachings of G. I. Gurdjieff and Rudolf Steiner. The practice itself is quite simple: before you go to bed each night, mentally retrace the events of your day. This exercise will help you to identify and correct your negative behaviors, attitudes, and reactions. I have found this simple practice to be very powerful; it has helped me become more conscious of my day-to-day behavior and the effect it has on others.

I lived in Minnesota while writing this book, and my partner was also working at home. During the long winter, we were cooped up together day after day, and we sometimes got on each other's nerves.

I have a temper, and just as I was about to let loose with an angry comment, I would abruptly stop when it occurred to me that I'd have to face my behavior in just a few short hours!

The exercise can be done in two distinct phases:

Phase One

Set aside at least five to fifteen minutes at the end of each day. Take a few deep breaths, and then mentally rewind the events of the day backward, starting with the most recent. Don't judge; simply observe the events of your day.

As you do this, you will become more conscious of your attitudes and behaviors. You will also clearly see the law of cause and effect at work—how everything we do, both positive and negative, will eventually show up in our own lives. If we gossip, someone will gossip about us. If we extend a kindness to someone, that will be returned to us as well. Practice phase one for a three- to six-month period before going on to the next phase.

Phase Two

As you review your day, ask yourself, "Was I harmless in my thoughts during this day? Was I harmless in my speech? Did I gossip or judge others? Was I harmless in my actions?" Again, don't judge or analyze; just be aware of your behavior and its effect on others. If you observe a negative behavior or reaction, ask yourself, "Could I have behaved differently?" Rewind the day, and imagine handling the situation again from the perspective of your higher self or soul. As you become more conscious of your patterns, you will notice that your day-to-day behavior will shift in subtle but important ways. You will start to self-correct as you become more conscious of your attitudes and reactions.

THE MENTAL BODY

When we want a more powerful computer, we upgrade it by installing more advanced hardware. When we refine the mental body, we are expanding our mental capabilities and upgrading our "receiving equipment." This upgrade makes it easier for information from the higher planes to reach our conscious awareness. The main tools used to refine this body are controlled thinking, meditation, and study.

Controlled thinking is practiced by directing our thoughts to spiritual values and ideas. This practice raises the vibration of the mental body, making it more receptive to subtle currents of thought. To practice controlled thinking, it is not necessary to suppress your thoughts. You need only to substitute a higher thought for a lower.

In *The Yoga Sutras*, Patanjali recommends that we follow a "mental diet" and choose our reading material with care.[19] In the modern world, this would include regulating our intake of other media—television, radio, and the internet—as well.

Meditation is the premiere method of refining the mental body. It is through meditation that we develop the ability to still the lower mind and make contact with the soul. The lower mind has been described as a "dark curtain" that blocks our access to the higher worlds.[20] When we still the lower mind, our focus of awareness shifts from the physical to the spiritual planes. The mind becomes receptive and alert, ready to do its job of transmitting information from the soul to the brain. In his book on the mental body, A. E. Powell writes, "Those who would deliberately undertake the task of bringing the higher consciousness into the brain may do so by a careful training of the lower mind. . . . The habit of quiet, sustained and sequential thought, directed to non-worldly subjects, of meditation, of study, develops the mental body and renders it a better instrument.

The effort to cultivate abstract thinking is also useful, thus raising the lower mind toward the higher."[21]

As you'll see in the next chapter, mind control is the first and most important step in any meditation practice. It is easy to focus our minds on something that interests or intrigues us but much harder to focus on a particular subject or object at will. In *The Silent Path*, Michal Eastcott recommends two basic focusing exercises to tune up and discipline the mind before starting a meditation practice. The goal is to train the mind to become our tool—our servant rather than our master.

Holding the Focus: Exercise 1

Pick an object—a building, a picture, or a shop window, for example—and carefully note every detail. Write down your precise observations and check for accuracy.

Holding the Focus: Exercise 2

In your mind's eye, visualize a familiar object or scene such as a household item, your garden, or your car. Hold the image for five minutes as you carefully add in each detail. Open your eyes and check for accuracy.

These deceptively simple but valuable practices will strengthen your ability to hold your point of focus where *you* choose, without the benefit of interest. Patanjali wrote that mastering the ability to concentrate on a physical object is essential before we turn our attention to the subtle worlds.[22]

Eastcott also addressed this issue when he wrote,

Abstract and spiritual matters have an intangible quality, which makes it genuinely hard for the mind to find something to take hold of, something it can focus on. There is often no ready point that it can grasp, and if it has not learned obedience to our directing will, there is little chance of it holding satisfactorily to such an elusive trail. Another reason is that spiritual concepts are often difficult, involving different processes of thought from the usual run; the mind must have a certain responsiveness to direction to work in this field with any ease . . . [the mind's] power to collaborate . . . will make it a controlled and sensitive instrument like a personal radar screen.[23]

We can make our daily lives an exercise in mind control by practicing *sati*, the Buddhist term for "mindfulness," in everything we do. To practice sati, also translated as "awareness" or "skillful attention," train your mind to stay focused on the present moment, rather than the past or the future, as you go about your day.

Study is the final tool. Through study we gain the intellectual framework we need to understand the Wisdom teachings. Study also helps us stretch our minds as we ponder the more abstract ideas and concepts.

One of the best techniques to cultivate abstract thinking is "seed-thought" meditation. In this type of meditation, we focus on a word, sentence, or symbol in an attempt to understand its deeper meaning. As we ponder its form, quality, purpose, and cause, we develop the ability to reach beyond the conscious mind to gain deeper insights.

In the next chapter, I will introduce you to the basic form of seed-thought meditation. But before you turn the page, I want to encourage you to create your own reading list of books that will stretch the boundaries of your conscious mind. Examples might include the book series by Alice Bailey, the Agni Yoga series by Helena Roerich, Patanjali's *Yoga Sutras*, the Bhagavad Gita, or an esoteric Christian text. When you ponder the content of these books, you are raising the vibration of your mental body and training your lower mind to think more abstractly.

Do you remember the legend of the Holy Grail? Legend has it that King Arthur sent his Knights of the Round Table from one end of Britain to the other in a quest to find this holy object. Dating back to the twelfth and thirteenth centuries, this legend has both Christian and Celtic roots. The Holy Grail has been described as a Celtic cauldron with magical powers, the chalice used by Jesus during the last supper, or, more recently, the womb of Mary Magdalene in books such as Michael Baigent's *Holy Blood, Holy Grail* and Dan Brown's bestseller, *The Da Vinci Code*. In the Arthurian legend, the Grail was a symbol of divine grace, available only to those who were spiritually prepared. After many tests and trials, it was only the saintly, Christ-like Sir Galahad who succeeded in finding it.

Rather than a sacred cup or magical cauldron, the Holy Grail is actually our purified physical, emotional, and mental bodies—the chalice we create to hold the light of our souls.

Chapter Six

BUILDING THE RAINBOW BRIDGE

To a mind that is still, the whole universe surrenders.

—Chuang-Tzu

The concept of a bridge that links the physical world with the world of spirit can be found in all our spiritual traditions, both ancient and modern. The ancient mystery tradition of Eleusis included an order of "bridge priestesses" who taught new initiates to build an inner bridge that would allow them to pass "from death to immorality." The name of their goddess was "the Lady of the Bridge."[1]

The Zoroastrians, followers of the great Iranian prophet Spitaman Zarathushtra, lived during the second millennium BCE. Their spiritual texts state that there is "a path that will be opened. . . . The bridge becometh a broad bridge for the righteous . . . and a narrow bridge for the wicked."[2] The Muslims speak of the bridge as being "thinner than a hair and sharper than a sword." They also believe that "a good man will be able to pass over the bridge, but the wicked will soon miss the footing and fall into hell."[3]

This concept is also part of the Aboriginal and Bushman cultures. The African Bushmen use medicine dances to build their bridge to the spirit world. During these ecstatic dances, their medicine men and women see "ropes to God," the vertical lines or strings of light that extend to the sky. Some Bushmen speak of floating into the sky when they see these ropes. Others experience the rope as a staircase or ladder. The rope is thought to extend from the tops of their heads upwards to the "Big God," who lives in the sky village with their ancestors.[4]

For the Aborigines, it is the mythical Rainbow Serpent who allows them entry into the invisible worlds. This serpent, when standing on her tail like a rainbow, connects the earth with the heavenly realms. Only an initiate of high degree is allowed to make contact with this serpent. The serpent is also a source of power for the Aborigines' medicine men. Their contact with the serpent allows them to enter the sky world in several ways. They can sit astride the serpent and ride into the heavens. They can also use it as a rope or ladder. In another version of this myth, the serpent transforms its back into a canoe, which allows them to paddle into the sky.[5]

In the Ageless Wisdom teachings, the bridge is called the Rainbow Bridge, or the Bridge of Light. In the Hindu texts, the bridge is called the *Antahkarana,* a Sanskrit word derived from *antah,* or "inner," and *karana,* or "instrument." This etheric bridge is our link between heaven and earth, our individual Jacob's Ladder. It links the lower mind with the higher, our individual consciousness with the universal consciousness of the soul. It is through this bridge that we bring creative ideas and spiritual wisdom down to earth. In the Christian tradition, the bridge is symbolized by the cross: the vertical beam represents our link with the higher worlds. In the New Testament, Jesus refers to this bridge as the "strait" or "narrow" gate (Matt. 7:13).

How do we construct this bridge? The well-known esoteric saying, "Before we can tread the spiritual path we must become that path," gives us a clue. Just as the spider spins its own web, the Rainbow Bridge is built with our own creative imagination. For this reason, the spider is sometimes found as a symbol in religious pictures and diagrams. In *The Secret Teachings of All Ages*, Manly Hall points out that Native American legends include a Spider Man whose web connects the heaven worlds with the earth. He also writes of the secret schools of India where mention was made of the Great Spider, the ruler of the Spider Gods, who created webs to connect the realms of darkness with the light.[6]

THE THREE THREADS

The threads that link us to our subtle bodies—the etheric, the emotional, and the lower mental—are created automatically through the evolutionary process. We now have to duplicate what God has done and consciously build a bridge to span the gaps that exist between the three aspects of the mind. As I mentioned, the Rainbow Bridge is built in two sections. The lower span is built between the rational mind, the highest aspect of the personality, and the soul. The higher span is built between the soul and the higher mind.

The threads that connect us to the soul include the life thread, anchored through the heart, and the consciousness thread, anchored in the head. These threads extend downward from the soul to the personality. There is a third thread that we ourselves generate: the creative thread, anchored in the throat center. This thread begins to form when the throat center becomes active.

Together, these three threads make up the Rainbow Bridge. This bridge is built as we project our attention upward from the personality to the soul.

The significance of these threads is honored in an ancient Hindu initiation ceremony. In India, candidates for initiation are given a sacred thread made up of three strands of yarn that are twisted, braided, and knotted into a circle. This thread, called a *yajnasutra*, symbolizes the thread that ties man to his soul. This thread is also called *tridandi*, for "three," which symbolizes the need to link the spirit, soul, and personality.[7] Initiates wear this thread over the left shoulder.

As I've mentioned, it is through our daily meditation that these threads fuse, blend, and widen as we slowly build a bridge of communication between the personality and the soul. It is at this point, in the words of the New Testament, that we "arise and go" back to the "Father's home" (Luke 15:18). The Rainbow Bridge, our ladder to the soul, is the "path of return."

Creative meditation is the tool we use to build this bridge. Many meditation practices focus only on quieting the mind. In creative meditation, we go a step further and actively train our minds to transmit information from the soul to the brain. In chapter 5, you learned to refine and raise the vibration of your physical, emotional, and mental bodies. The practice of creative meditation will help you to further refine and "weld" these bodies into a cohesive whole. You will then have a clear, unobstructed channel for the free flow of information from the soul to the brain. Over time, this type meditation will also result in the transfer of energy from the lower centers to the higher.

As you saw in chapter 3, this teaching lies at the heart of all our spiritual traditions, and the same basic method is used in both the East and the West.

HEART AND HEAD

Our great Christian mystics have left us with vivid descriptions of the mystical experience. Through prayer and devotion, they contact God in a moment of ecstasy, and they long for the continuation of that rapturous experience. Darkness descends as they lose their contact with the Divine. One very poignant example of this experience can be found in the letters of Mother Teresa.

Born Agnes Gonxha Bojaxhiu in 1910 in modern-day Macedonia, Mother Teresa was known as "the Saint of the Gutters." She became a nun in 1928 and spent her early years teaching school in Calcutta. In 1946, while riding on a train to the mountain town of Darjeeling, she received a calling from Christ "to serve him among the poorest of the poor." She began her work in 1948 and eventually founded the Missionaries of Charity, a worldwide network of orphanages, hospices, and other charity centers.

Her contact with the Christ continued through the early years of her mission, and it was during this time that she wrote, "My soul at present is in perfect peace and joy." Two years later, despite her deep longing, her contact with the Christ abruptly stopped. She wrote to her advisors despairingly of the "terrible darkness" within her. During the last fifty years of her life, with the exception of one brief respite, she longed for but did not experience the presence of Christ. In a series of letters written to her superiors and published under the title *Mother Teresa: Come Be My Light*, she documents her torment and spiritual pain. "The silence and the emptiness is so great—that I look and do not see, listen and do not hear. . . . I call, I cling, I want—and there is no one to answer."[8]

Mother Teresa's writings illustrate the duality inherent in the mystical experience—the separation between the mystic and an often-elusive God. The mystic uses the heart center to make contact with the higher worlds. The esotericist adds the mind to the heart-centered way of the mystic. This enables us to do more than briefly touch the higher worlds; we use the mind to enter into and *become a part* of that world. The illusion of duality disappears as we experience our essential unity.

The word *esoteric* is derived from the Greek word *esoterikos,* or "inner." Webster's dictionary defines *esoteric* as "understood by or meant for only the elect few who have special knowledge or interest." In the ancient world, only initiates had access to these teachings. Today, esoteric training is self-initiated and self-imposed. It is up to us to decide if and when we are ready to commit to the daily discipline this training requires. Like an athlete who slowly builds strength and muscle by lifting weights every day, we become mental athletes as we train our minds, step by step, to access ever higher and more subtle realms of thought. As Michal Eastcott wrote,

> Meditation has been compared to sending a missile into outer space. . . . We are literally shooting off from our earthbound station when we direct the consciousness upwards in meditation. Like a satellite leaving the launching pad, we are probing out to areas not yet sign-posted, to regions far beyond those that are known. . . . It is truly a science of "inner space" [in the same way that] astrophysics is the science of the outer cosmic realm. . . . In line with all scientific procedure, it is a deliberate, controlled, step by step process . . . a method of progressing in consciousness through various states or stages.[9]

There are five stages of creative meditation: concentration, meditation, contemplation, illumination, and inspiration. As I mentioned in the last chapter, the first and most important steps are concentration and mind control.

THE STAGES OF CREATIVE MEDITATION

The word *concentration,* from the Latin *con,* or "together," and *centrare,* or "center," is defined as "bringing together" or drawing to a "focal point."

Another definition of concentration is "one-pointed attention," the ability to focus and hold our attention on an object or thought at will.

It is through mind control that we learn to withdraw our attention from the outer world and gradually refocus and reorient it to the subtle realms. When we do this, the mind becomes our true sixth sense. Our physical senses are constantly telegraphing information about the physical world to the brain. In the same way, the mind can be trained to relay information from the subtle realms to the brain. A new world then opens up before us.

As you saw in the last chapter, concentration practices can include basic focusing exercises; they can also include mantra meditations, in which we focus the mind on a particular word or phrase. In the raja yoga method, we use the seed-thought meditation I'll describe below.

This is the longest and most difficult stage, as we slowly gain control of the mind. Discipline, regularity, and patient persistence are the keys. The discipline of mind control is emphasized in all contemplative traditions. In the Bhagavad Gita, Arjuna cries, "The mind wavers, Krisha. Turbulent, impetuous, forceful, I think it is as hard to hold as the wind!" Krishna replies: "Without doubt . . . the wavering mind is hard to hold; but through assiduous practice . . . it may be held firm. For him whose mind is uncontrolled, union is hard to obtain . . . but for him whose mind has been brought under his sway, who is controlled, it may be won."[10]

In *Concentration and Meditation*, the Buddhist scholar Christmas Humphreys quotes a student: "Before one can meditate, one must learn to concentrate; otherwise one will be possessed with the will and inspiration but lack the necessary third ingredient—technique." Humphreys compares concentration practices to a ballet dancer doing exercises before performing a dance or a young pianist practicing scales.[11]

On the subject of mind control, the fourteenth-century German theologian and mystic Meister Eckhart wrote that "St. Paul reminds us that we, being planted in the likeness of God, may attain to higher and truer vision. For this Dionysius says we require three things. The first is, possession of one's mind. The second is, a mind that is free. The third is, a mind that can see. How can we acquire this speculative mind? By a habit of mental concentration."[12]

In *The Yoga Sutras*, Patanjali defines *dharana*, or "concentration," as "holding the mind within a center of spiritual consciousness . . . or fixing it on some divine form, either within the body or outside it." True concentration, he writes, is achieved when we can hold the mind to one thought for a period of twelve seconds. *Dhyana*, or meditation, is simply prolonged concentration, the ability to hold our attention, in any direction, on a particular idea or thought.[13]

The transition from meditation to contemplation has been described as passing from "meditation with seed to meditation without seed."[14] The mind remains focused, but instead of intense mental activity, we simply wait as the mind, shut off from the outer world, is now reoriented to the subtle worlds. The two stages of meditation, one of intense activity and the other of quiet waiting, have been called the "Mary and Martha states," a reference to the symbolic New Testament story of Jesus's visit to two sisters—one distracted by household tasks, the other who sits quietly at his feet.

The stage of contemplation is reached when we make contact with the soul. When we hold our minds "steady in the light," the mind can be impressed with the wisdom and knowledge of the soul. In the Wisdom teachings, this stage is called the "higher interlude."[15]

Our souls are *en rapport* with the universal mind, the storehouse of all wisdom and knowledge. Through the soul, we have access to all knowledge, past, present, and future. When we make contact with the soul, we also have the ability to communicate telepathically with the souls of others. This allows us to work with the higher beings that guide the evolution of our planet. At its highest, this experience has resulted in the transmission of our world scriptures, as outlined in chapter 4.

Once information and ideas from the soul are impressed on the mind, this process is repeated as the mind relays the information to the brain. As Alice Bailey put it in her wonderful book *From Intellect to Intuition*, "The mind receives illumination from the soul, in the form of ideas thrown into it, or of intuitions which convey exact and direct knowledge. . . . This process is in turn repeated by the active mind, which throws down into the receptive brain the intuitions and knowledge the soul has transmitted."[16]

Illumination is achieved when the information from the soul registers in the brain. This is a slow process, developed over time. As Bailey continues, "The flashes . . . are at first simply vivid flashes of illumination, breaking forth into the mind and disappearing almost instantaneously. But they come with increasing frequency, as the habit of meditation is cultivated and persist for increasingly long periods as stability of the mind is achieved. Gradually the light shines forth in a continuous stream."[17]

Inspiration occurs as we, like the famous creative artists and scientists in chapter 4, utilize the information we receive in the arts, science, business, or other service. The downpouring of energy from the soul to the brain awakens new brain cells, and creative leaps and inspired thinking can occur.

RAJA YOGA MEDITATION

Success with creative, or raja yoga, meditation relies on two things: persistence and regularity. It's better to meditate ten minutes per day than an hour once a week. Morning is always the best time, before your mind becomes engaged with the tasks of the day.

I am as far from a morning person as anyone can be. I like to wake up slowly and gently ease into the day. For me, the ideal day includes time to drink a cup of tea and read in bed for a while before I begin my day. For most of my adult life, I was involved with the deadline-driven world of magazine publishing and had to jump out of bed as soon as the alarm went off and hit the ground running.

During the years I worked on this book, I had an extended period when I could finally honor my natural rhythms. Even though I knew that it was best to meditate first thing in the morning, I didn't want to jump out of bed and start training my mind as soon as I opened my eyes. I wanted to fully enjoy my leisurely morning. There was one problem—my lovely, leisurely morning gave me too much time to think about the day ahead; by the time I was ready to meditate, I was already thinking about the things I needed to do and I struggled to quiet my mind.

I tried a variety of things and finally found a solution that worked for me: after I wake up, I stay in bed and read the newspaper for about twenty minutes. This gives me time to slowly wake up but not enough time for my mind to focus on the day ahead. Before I get up, I read everything from editorials to movie reviews to Dear Abby. I'm sure I'd be thrown out of any ashram in the world, but it works for me.

Find a rhythm that works for you, one that you can stick with over time. Some people meditate immediately upon rising; others take a shower and get dressed before they begin. Always meditate in the same spot. This will allow a vibration to build up that will make it easier for you to shift into a deeper state. You don't need a special room, but find a spot where you can create a tiny "temple" of your own. I meditate on a couch in my home office, next to a small altar and book shelf. I've had several houseguests meditate with me, and they've all remarked on how easy it was to meditate deeply there.

As you experiment with this meditation, remember that full soul consciousness is an advanced state that can take years—or even lifetimes—to achieve. Even so, you may be surprised, as I was, at how quickly you will feel a deepening connection to your soul. In the New Testament letter The Epistle of James, the author writes, "Draw near to God, and he will draw near to you" (James 4:8). In the same way, when we focus our attention upward, the soul turns its attention downward. The Rainbow Bridge is built through the *united* effort of both the soul and the personality. As we continue to project our attention upward, we anchor small threads of energy that will eventually, thread by thread, form an inner stairway to the higher worlds. As we approach the soul, we increasingly come under the influence of its higher vibration, and our own vibratory rate starts to speed up.

Our peak experiences—those moments of deep compassion and forgiveness, of love, joy, serenity, and intuitive understanding—are all expressions of the soul. The goal of our daily practice is to increase these moments until we are living in full communion with our souls each and every day.

It is through our unwavering dedication to our daily practice that we, in the words of the Bible, "take heaven by storm" (Matt. 11:12). It is our determination to stick with the long, often tedious, stage of mind control that will eventually open the door to the higher worlds. When the vibratory rate of our mind and brain matches that of the soul, it becomes possible to enter the higher worlds at will.

As human beings, it is our privilege to reveal this new and subtle world. Like Christopher Columbus, Magellan, and other explorers of the physical world, we are pioneers venturing into new and uncharted territory. We are blazing a trail, creating a map of the subtle world that others can follow.

SEED THOUGHTS

As I mentioned in the last chapter, seed-thought meditation includes the use of a sentence, word, or symbol. In this type of meditation, we meditate on the form, quality, purpose, and cause of each seed thought. This technique is used to increase our powers of concentration and to train our minds to think more abstractly. I have found Bailey's recommendation for working with seed thoughts to be very helpful: "Imagine that you have to give a lecture upon these words to an audience. Picture yourself as formulating the notes upon which you will later speak. As you carry your mind from stage to stage, you will find that ten minutes will have gone by without your attention wavering, so great will have been your interest."[18]

Before you experiment with the meditation below, remember that the downpouring of subtle energy is always stimulating to the brain. If you have trouble sleeping, it may be a sign that you are meditating too long or too often. If that's the case, stop your meditation practice until your sleep patterns are restored. The meditations in this book should never exceed thirty minutes and should never be practiced more than once per day.

Below is the basic form of raja yoga meditation, adapted from the Lucis Trust, a nonprofit educational organization started by Alice and Foster Bailey.[19] This meditation will help you to develop the basic powers of concentration you'll need to build your bridge to the soul. Practice this meditation for six months before moving on to the more advanced meditations in the next chapter.

1. Give yourself fifteen minutes of uninterrupted quiet time. Calm yourself by closing your eyes and following your breath, in and out, for a count of ten.

2. When you are ready, use your creative imagination to lift your consciousness to a focal point outside and above your head. See this as the analytical, lower mind, now still and receptive. Project a line of light upwards to the soul center, six inches above your head. See it as a brilliant sun, a radiant source of energy.

3. Visualize this line of light reaching even higher, toward the higher, or intuitive, mind. Take a moment to hold this lighted alignment.

4. Pause for a moment as you experience the light and energy of your soul. Then, holding the mind steady in the light, meditate for ten to fifteen minutes on one of the seed thoughts below. Examine the words first with the analytical mind. Carry your thought as far as you can in analysis and analogy as you seek to penetrate the inner meaning.

5. To end your meditation, visualize a pure white light pouring down from your soul, illuminating your mind, calming your emotions, and invigorating your physical body. Acting as a channel for the transmission of energy and as an act of service to humanity, pour out the energies released during the meditation process. Use the Great Invocation below to circulate light, love, and power throughout the world.

THE GREAT INVOCATION

The Great Invocation is a world prayer that has been translated into more than seventy-five languages and dialects. Use this prayer daily as an act of service to humanity. As you say the invocation, visualize spiritual light and love entering the hearts and minds of all people in every corner of the globe.

Remember that our focused, united intentions can literally change the world. Corinne McLaughlin and Gordon Davidson have pointed out that thousands of copies of the Great Invocation were distributed in the Philippines during the nonviolent People Power Revolution that led to the ouster of President Ferdinand Marcos. The invocation was repeated daily after the departure of Marcos and hourly on the day that new elections were held that restored the country's democratic government.[20]

Also, remember that the Sanskrit word *manas*, or "man," refers not to gender but to "one who thinks." The word *Christ* refers to the world teacher of all religions, not just Christianity. This prayer was first published during World War II; the word *evil* refers to the great conflict of that time.

The Great Invocation

From the point of Light within the Mind of God
Let light stream forth into the minds of men.
Let Light descend on Earth.

From the point of Love within the Heart of God
Let love stream forth into the hearts of men.
May Christ return to Earth.

From the center where the Will of God is known
Let purpose guide the little wills of men—
The purpose which the Masters know and serve.

From the center which we call the race of men
Let the Plan of Love and Light work out
And may it seal the door where evil dwells.

Let Light and Love and Power restore the Plan on Earth.[21]

SEED THOUGHTS

Meditate on each of the following seed thoughts for a period of one month:

1. Let the actions of my soul motivate my daily life.

2. I stand within the light, and as the light shines through my form, I radiate that light.

3. Through the soul, the law of love is manifested.

4. With self-forgetfulness, I gather what I need for the helping of my fellowmen.

5. The keywords of my life are stability, serenity, strength, and service.

6. The will of the soul becomes my will.

THE VOICE OF THE SOUL

In the early 1960s, Eileen Caddy was meditating in a small chapel in Glastonbury, England, when she suddenly heard a "voice" inside her head. Over the next several years, the voice she called "the God within" provided step-by-step instructions that led to the founding of the Findhorn community in a remote corner of northeast Scotland. There she, her husband, Peter, and their friend Dorothy Maclean created their famous gardens with the aid of nature spirits and devas. In doing so, they demonstrated to the world the value of inner listening and a life led in conscious cooperation with beings from the subtle worlds.[22]

Steve Nation, the New York director of the Lucis Trust, is a long-time student of the Wisdom teachings and the cofounder of Intuition in Service, a website that provides articles and meditations on spiritual intuition and world service. Nation was a nineteen-year-old college student in Napier, New Zealand, when he picked up a Lucis Trust pamphlet at a committee meeting. "I was suddenly jolted by an electric shock that went from the top of my head down to the bottom of my feet," Nation said. "It was the strangest feeling. . . . Nothing like that had ever happened to me before." He was introduced to the Bailey teachings soon after, and he joined the Arcane School at age twenty-two. Nation says that the Arcane School disciplines of meditation and study provided "a structure, a spiritual practice and stable center that eventually made me into an entirely different person." Discipline and persistence are the keys, he says, and the payoff is the relationship we build with our souls. "When the soul becomes a real part of our lives, everything changes. We see life from a higher altitude and more easily understand spiritual concepts—concepts don't always make sense to the personality."

His meditation practice has also changed the way he views the world. "Meditation has made me sensitive to the inner realities," Nation says. "I know a lot of wonderful people who are depressed about the state of the world today. What I see is an extraordinary renaissance of spiritual thinking and an awakening of the spiritual will in human affairs. I see the evidence all around me of a new humanity being born. My life has been shaped by my contact with the Bailey teachings," he says, "but this work is just one expression of a universal teaching that enables us to build a relationship with our souls."[23]

Steven Lumiere was also nineteen when he attended a lecture by an alternative healer who suddenly pointed to him and said, "You are a natural healer, and you should be working in this field." He started a meditation practice soon after and eventually received information about new healing techniques. As he explained, "As I was meditating, information from my higher self or soul suddenly flooded into my brain. I saw the true nature of reality—that everything is energy and that divinity is inherent in all things. I discovered that I could see into a client's energy field and clear their chakras and energy systems with just my intention. As time went on, I began to receive instruction from higher beings—master teachers who taught me to use my higher facilities to access and step down pure levels of information." For the last thirty-three years, Steven has maintained a full-time healing practice. He works with people all over the world on a variety of physical and psychological issues including cancer, chronic fatigue syndrome, autoimmune disorders, trauma, and depression.[24]

A NEW WAY OF LEARNING

While working on this book, I had an interesting dream. I dreamt that I was working on a big project that entailed collecting, organizing, and filing written materials. I was under deadline pressure and feeling a little anxious. I was working steadily but slowly, because I was blind. At a certain point, it dawned on me that I wasn't really blind, that it was possible to work more quickly and efficiently—I just hadn't realized that I could actually see.

The message of the dream seemed obvious in light of what I was learning. By then I had put years into a slow, laborious study of this complicated and subtle topic.

The information we need for any book or project is already present in the subtle worlds that surround us. Our broadband computer networks have made it possible to access information from anywhere in the world with a few simple keystrokes. The next frontier is the discovery and utilization of the "etheric broadband" that will give us immediate access to an even greater storehouse of information. Like Ali Baba in the *Arabian Nights*, we will open the door to a treasure trove of unimaginable riches.

At present, the intellect is thought to be the pinnacle of human development, and our educational system is geared to the training and development of the lower mind. The Wisdom teachings tell us that the education of the future will include the Science of the *Antahkarana*—what Bailey calls the "new and true" science of the mind.[25] This science will include the bridge-building techniques that will teach children to access information by direct, intuitive means.

As we've seen, at an earlier stage of our development, instinct was our primary means of accessing information. Instinctual knowledge was eventually superseded by the higher faculty of rational knowing. Our instinctual knowing is still present within us, but it now operates beneath the threshold of our conscious awareness; it makes itself known in our gut feelings about the people and circumstances in our lives.

As we take the next step up the evolutionary ladder and develop the ability to reach beyond the lower mind, our rational way of knowing will also slip beneath the threshold of our conscious awareness, still present but superseded by the new and higher way of accessing information.

The ability to enter the subtle worlds at will is the high prize and ultimate goal of esoteric training. This development will allow us to access the mind of God and directly register what the Bible calls "the pattern of things in the heavens"—the blueprint of the cosmos (Heb. 9:23). We will then understand and be able to participate consciously in the great plan for humanity. Bailey addressed this step when she wrote,

> One after another the sons [and daughters] of God have entered into their heritage and found themselves sensitive to the world plan. They have, through steadfastness in contemplation, equipped themselves to act as interpreters of the Universal Mind and as intermediaries between the non-telepathic multitudes and the eternal fountain of wisdom. To the illuminates of the world, to the intuitive thinkers in all fields of knowledge, and to the telepathic and inspired communicators can be traced the best that man now knows.[26]

Our repeated contact with these higher worlds will, in the end, produce a new type of human: the soul-aligned human being. In the next chapter I will cover the Wisdom teachings on soul alignment.

Chapter Seven

THE SOUL: THE KINGDOM OF GOD

We see the world piece by piece, as the sun, the moon, the animal, the tree; but the whole, of which these are the shining parts, is the soul.

—Ralph Waldo Emerson

Throughout history there have been many examples of soul-aligned human beings. As Corinne McLaughlin and Gordon Davidson have pointed out in their book *Spiritual Politics*, these examples range from statesmen like Abraham Lincoln; religious leaders like the Jesus and the Buddha; philosophers such as Pythagoras, Socrates, and Plato; scientists such as Louis Pasteur and Albert Einstein; artists such as Michelangelo and Leonard da Vinci; and humanitarians like Albert Schweitzer and Florence Nightingale.[1] Gandhi, who used what he called "soul force" during the Indian independence movement, was called a *mahatma*, a man of "great soul."

THE CHRIST

Jesus is the purest example we have in the West of the soul in full manifestation. In the gospel stories, he demonstrated the soul qualities of love, compassion, tolerance, and forgiveness. As the spiritual teacher White Eagle put it, "Jesus the Christ is a master soul, man made perfect; this highly evolved and perfected soul incarnated in order to reveal to individual man what he could himself attain if he followed the simple, gentle way of the Christ."[2]

According to the Wisdom teachings, it was Jesus's task to anchor the first threads of the Kingdom of God on earth, and this subject was the focus of his ministry. In his sermons, he spoke of a kingdom that was "not of this world" (John 18:36), one not accessible by "flesh and blood" (1 Cor. 15:50). He repeatedly stated that this kingdom is "within our midst" (Luke 17:21). And the Lord's Prayer, the one prayer he urged his followers to use, contains the words, "Thy kingdom come, Thy will be done, on earth, as it is in heaven."

The New Testament is one of three books—the other two being *The Yoga Sutras* and the Hindu bible, the Bhagavad Gita—that contain the complete story of the unfolding human soul. This process unfolds in a series of five graded steps, called initiations. In the New Testament, Jesus modeled the dramatic story of these five initiations: the birth at Bethlehem, symbolizing control of the physical body and the birth of the Christ within; baptism, symbolizing our control over the emotional body; transfiguration, symbolizing our control over the mental body and the union with our souls; the Crucifixion, which symbolizes the "death" of the lower self and our entrance into the Kingdom of God; and the Resurrection and Ascension, which symbolizes the full expression of our divinity and the completion of our evolutionary journey.[3]

When we make contact with the soul, we take our first steps into the spiritual kingdom. In the Bible, the Christ said, "Let your lights shine" (Matt. 5:16); and, in the Wisdom teachings, this step is called the "lighting of the lamp."[4] Eventually, the little light of the personality gives way and is engulfed by the greater light of the soul. The soul and the personality merge and become one.

The teaching on soul alignment can be found in several Bible verses and, more explicitly, in the gnostic Gospels:

"The first man is of the earth, earthy; the second [the soul or higher] man is the Lord from heaven" (1 Cor. 15:47).

In aligning the personality with the soul, we "make out of twain, one new man" (Eph. 2:15).

In the Gospel of Thomas, Jesus makes several references to soul alignment: "When you make the two into one . . . you will enter the kingdom."[5] "Blessed are the solitary . . . for you will find the kingdom. For you are from it, and to it you will return."[6] "There are many standing at the door, but only those who are solitary will enter."[7]

The concept of the soul can be found in all cultures and spiritual traditions. For the ancient Egyptians, the soul had three intertwined elements, or aspects, called the *ka, ba,* and *khu.* The ka was seen as the animating life-force or vital essence. The ba, for "noble" or "sublime," was usually depicted as a bird with a human head; this aspect of soul could travel between the worlds of the living and the dead. The khu, the third aspect of the soul, was considered to be the divine intelligence or spiritual body. In Judaism, there are also three words that roughly translate as "soul" or "spirit": *nephesh, ruach,* and *neshamah.* Nephesh is the life force; ruach, the divine spirit. Neshamah is the bridge between human and divine realms.

The ancient Greeks made the first philosophical study of the soul. Plato, an initiate of the Egyptian mystery schools, defined the soul as "the essence of being." His disciple Aristotle viewed the soul as a substance, "the cause or source of the living body." In Hinduism the divine element in man is called the *atman,* or "self." In Buddhism, the soul is the "middle principle," that which connects the lower and higher worlds.

For most of our time on earth, we identify with our physical bodies and experience what Buddhists call the "great heresy"—the illusion that we are individualized, separate beings. When we awaken to the soul within, we realize that we are part of a great universal life, the soul of humanity; we find our place within the greater whole and experience our interconnection with all life. Our sense of separation disappears, as one author put it, "like fog in the sunshine."[8]

When we experience our essential oneness, we never look at life in the same way again. Bill Bauman, a spiritual teacher living in Las Vegas, is a former Catholic priest with degrees in philosophy, theology, and psychology. Bauman has worked as a psychologist, a business consultant, and a peace activist. Heart-centered but secretly proud of his scientific bent and intellectual prowess, he was startled one day to get this intuitive message: "Let go of your beliefs, theories and intelligent interpretations about life. Forget everything you've ever learned!" After some resistance, he decided to act on this message. Every time his mind presented him with a theory or belief, he ignored it and focused instead on his experience of life from moment to moment.

As his mind began to quiet down, he experienced a new level of being. As he writes in his book *Soul Vision*, "Something deeper and fuller happened within me. . . . I stopped feeling so separate from others and from life. . . . Living became more and more an experience of the heart and the soul. A feeling of oneness filled my awareness. . . . I saw the human race as the human family, humanity and the environment as one earthly presence and the divine and the human as an interconnected reality."[9]

As time went on, his experience deepened and he began living in a state he calls "pure being." As he puts it, "Once again, my whole relationship with the earth and the human race changed. . . . I now began living in the middle of humanity's soul and perceived all of the human experience through its essence-centered eyes. . . . As I got used to living in life's essence, I found myself experiencing a remarkable quality of inner peace, more profound and real than any I have ever known."[10] Bauman has since made it his mission to share his expanded vision of life and to help others awaken to their divine nature.

Our inherent sense of oneness and interconnection can make itself known even in the midst of war. One cold and snowy night in Minnesota, I was watching the History Channel when I saw and was very touched by a documentary about the World War 1 Christmas Truce.

In December 1914, six months after the start of the war, more than one million soldiers had died, and many more were wounded. The opposing armies—German troops on one side and English, French, and Belgian troops on the other—were dug into trenches on the western front, from the North Sea coast to the Swiss border. The close proximity of the trenches, only fifty to one thousand yards apart, allowed each side to hear occasional bits of conversation and laughter.

The truce began on Christmas Eve, when German soldiers placed makeshift Christmas trees with lighted candles above their trenches in the area around Ypres, Belgium. After they sang "Silent Night," English soldiers clapped and responded by singing a Christmas carol of their own. Soon, Christmas greetings were exchanged, and both sides crossed the "no man's land" between the trenches, shook hands, and exchanged gifts of food, cigarettes, and coffee.

On Christmas day, the English and German soldiers conducted both separate and joint burial services for their fallen comrades. English soldiers butchered a pig and shared their Christmas dinner with the Germans, who supplied the beer. Amateur photos taken that day show relaxed groups of English and German soldiers smiling for the cameras. The Christmas exchanges also included belts, buttons, and uniform badges. As one British lieutenant later wrote, "I spotted a German officer, some sort of lieutenant I should think, and being a bit of a collector, I intimated to him that I had taken a fancy to some of his buttons. . . . I brought out my wire clippers and, with a few deft snips, removed a couple of his buttons and put them in my pocket. I then gave him two of mine in exchange." He added, "The last I saw was one of my machine gunners, who was a bit of an amateur hairdresser in civil life, cutting the unnaturally long hair of a docile Boche, who was patiently kneeling on the ground whilst the automatic clippers crept up the back of his neck." A German soldier later wrote home that "it was a Christmas celebration in keeping with the command 'Peace on earth' and a memory which will stay with us always."[11]

As night approached, the men began drifting back to their trenches. As one British private wrote in his diary, "Altogether we had a great day with our enemies, and parted with much handshaking and mutual goodwill."[12]

Hundreds of such truces, involving over one hundred thousand British and German troops, spontaneously occurred along the western front that day. Outraged by these unofficial truces, both the English and German High Command ordered their soldiers to resume the fight, but, in many areas, the soldiers on both sides were reluctant to give up the peace. On December 26, a German officer met with his British counterpart to warn him that he had orders to resume the hostilities. Soon after, a message was thrown into a British trench that read, "We shoot to the air," and later, a few badly aimed, high shots were fired over the British trenches. In another area, when German officers ordered their men to shoot, the men simply refused.

As a German soldier later said, "The officers stormed up and down and got, as the only answer, 'We can't—they are good fellows—we can't.'" After being repeatedly threatened, they reluctantly fired, but again, they aimed high over the British trenches. As one man remembered, "We spent that day and the next wasting ammunition trying to shoot the stars down from the sky."[13] This event marks the only time in history that a truce spontaneously arose from the lower ranks in the middle of war.

Another good illustration concerns the friendship between two opposing fighter pilots. In 1972, Major Dan Cherry was an Air Force fighter pilot serving in Vietnam. While on a combat mission near Hanoi, Major Cherry shot down a fighter jet piloted by Lieutenant Nguyen Hong My after a fierce, five-minute air battle. Cherry watched as the pilot opened his parachute after jumping from his burning plane. After the war, Major Cherry often wondered what had happened to the Vietnamese pilot. Thirty years later, while visiting the National Museum of the US Air Force in Dayton, Ohio, Cherry came across the plane he had piloted that day. Seeing the plane caused Cherry to wonder, once again, what had happened to the brave pilot who had parachuted from that plane.

With the help of a Vietnamese television producer, Cherry was able to track down his former adversary. They met in Ho Chi Minh City and instantly recognized their common humanity. A fast friendship developed, and Cherry accepted Hong My's invitation to fly to Hanoi to meet his wife and children. When the Vietnamese pilot and his son visited the United States in 2009, Cherry and Hong My shared their story at a variety of aviation-related events.

As Cherry wrote in his 2009 book, *My Enemy, My Friend: A Story of Reconciliation from the Vietnam War*, "It felt strange flying on Vietnam Airlines over the same countryside where I had flown countless combat missions. Only this time, my former adversary was by my side. . . . Mr. Hong My and I both share the mutual hope that our unusual friendship can help Vietnam veterans bring closure to their wartime experience . . . and inspire our two countries to work toward better and friendlier relations."[14]

CONTACTING THE SOUL

The soul, the repository of our many lifetimes of experience, is our most reliable source of direction and guidance. It is our divine partner, an internal GPS system that guides our lives, first as subtle promptings and later, as we establish a deeper connection, as a source of wisdom we can contact at will. In the past, it has been only the "special" people— our mystics, seers, and saints—who have spoken of this experience. Today, there are many people, in a variety of fields, who work under the direct guidance of their souls.

LaUna Huffines is the author of two books on the Wisdom tradition—*Bridge of Light: Tools of Light for Spiritual Transformation* and *Healing Yourself with Light: How to Connect with the Angelic Healers*. According to Huffines, her books have been written in partnership with her soul. "The soul is much wiser and more powerful; when we get in touch with the will of our souls, it streams energy to us and enables us to do things beyond the goals of the personality. When I begin a book, I sit down with a digital recorder and wait until the information is given to me. It's only when my mind is still and silent that the information will come through. I focus all my energy on receiving the information as purely as possible." Huffines believes that we can connect with the soul by dedicating ourselves to our spiritual purpose and by desiring the soul's wisdom more than anything else.

She recommends using the powerful "as if" technique: "Wake up and say, today I will think as the soul, speak as the soul, and live as the soul. If you do this persistently, the link to your soul will be established."[15]

.Nancy Seifer is the coauthor of *When the Soul Awakens: The Path to Spiritual Evolution and a New World Era.* With her husband and coauthor, Martin Vieweg, she manages a website that provides a wide range of articles on the Wisdom teachings and is involved in esoteric group work. In the late 1960s, after a stint in the Peace Corps and a job in community development, Seifer was drawn into the political campaign of a charismatic young mayor. She later joined his staff, but soon became disillusioned with the broken promises and political corruption she saw. In 1977, following several years at a think tank, she decided to take a six-month break to think about her next career move. For years she had kept track of her appointments in a Week-at–a-Glance datebook and had developed the habit of writing down her experiences at the end of each day.

After leaving her job, as she pondered the deeper meaning of her life, she began to record her inner experiences in a journal. To her surprise, the experience was life changing. "Once I started writing," she told me, "I began to receive an outpouring of information that was clearly beyond anything I knew consciously. I filled notebook after notebook and eventually realized that I was receiving insights from my soul—and from higher beings. The information ranged from insights about my own life to the deeper meaning of world events. I was soon writing all day, every day; I knew that something huge was unfolding in my life and that I needed to stay with it."

During this time, she began to attend conferences on spiritual topics and soon became a student of the Wisdom teachings. "As my awareness of the spiritual world increased, my soul began to play a greater and greater role in my life. I would pose questions and write down the answers as they were telepathically transmitted. I trusted the guidance I received and began to follow it in all aspects of my life. Out of this guidance came *When the Soul Awakens*. A lot of the content came from the inner flow I had developed from the decades of inner listening."[16]

Seifer's husband, Martin Vieweg, lectures for a variety of esoteric organizations. "I have the experience of being guided when I'm engaged in active service," he told me. "Once the bridge to the soul is built, it's like pressing the right key on your keyboard—the information is there when you need it." He added, "When we become a conduit for spiritual energy, we see the laws of synchronicity at work. We find ourselves in the right place at the right time with the right people saying the right things because we've learned to stand in spiritual being— it's like being in the zone."[17]

And during my conversation with Steve Nation, he added, "Part of what I see and do comes from the soul. Writing is much easier now than it used to be. Once I focus my mind on a task, the soul brings the ideas forward. The content is way beyond my personal self; it has an authority I know is not mine." Laying the groundwork first is important, Nation says, as it stimulates the release of information from the soul. "When we do the research and take care of the details beforehand, we create an evocative environment for the soul to use. We have to remember it's a co-creation."[18]

SOUL-ALIGNMENT MEDITATION

The following meditation was adapted from the Lucis Trust. It can be used each morning to align your physical, emotional, and mental bodies with the soul. Practice this meditation for three to six months before moving on to the more advanced meditation that follows. The *Om* used below is an ancient word used to still the three lower bodies.

1. Give yourself fifteen minutes of uninterrupted quiet time. Calm yourself by closing your eyes and following your breath, in and out, for a count of ten.

2. Focus your attention in the center of your head, in the region near the pineal gland.

3. Using your imagination, extend your consciousness upward in three stages:

   a. From the physical brain to the emotional body.
   b. From the emotional body to the lower mind. Pause for a moment to experience yourself as an integrated personality.
   c. From the integrated personality to the soul.

4. While keeping your consciousness focused in the center of your head, see a thread of golden light connecting your three bodies. Imagine this thread as three intertwined cables extending from the heart, throat, and head centers connecting you—the personality—with your soul. When you have carried it upward and have seen it aligning all aspects of the personality, pause in your meditation and realize that you are now face to face with your soul.

5. Sound the *Om* and silently repeat the following mantra:

> I am the soul,
> I am the light divine.
> I am love, I am will,
> I am fixed design.

6. Meditate on one of the monthly seed thoughts below for ten to fifteen minutes.

7. Sound the *Om* again silently. Visualize a pure white light pouring down from your soul, illuminating your mind, calming your emotions, and invigorating your physical body. Send out this incoming light and love to your fellow servers, your family and friends, and all those in need of healing.

8. Sound the *Om* again and inwardly say, "May the light of my soul guide and direct my actions on this day." Repeat the Great Invocation below.

The Great Invocation

From the point of Light within the Mind of God
Let light stream forth into the minds of men.
Let Light descend on Earth.

From the point of Love within the Heart of God
Let love stream forth into the hearts of men.
May Christ return to Earth.

From the center where the Will of God is known
Let purpose guide the little wills of men
The purpose which the Masters know and serve.

From the center which we call the race of men
Let the Plan of Love and Light work out
And may it seal the door where evil dwells.

Let Light and Love and Power restore the Plan on Earth.

SEED THOUGHTS

Use each seed thought for a period of one month:

1. I am a point of light within a greater light.

2. In silence, I hear the voice of my soul.

3. Let the radiance of my heart be a gift to others.

4. The way to direct knowledge is through alignment.

5. Union with my soul is the pearl of great price.

6. My obstacles are possibilities.

MEDITATION ON HIGHER GUIDANCE

This meditation has also been adapted from Lucis Trust. Use it to strengthen the alignment of your soul, mind, and brain. This alignment will make the higher interlude, in which the mind becomes receptive to impressions from the soul, and the lower interlude, in which the brain becomes receptive to impressions from the mind, possible. Keep a journal nearby to record any intuitions or information you receive.

1. Give yourself fifteen minutes of uninterrupted quiet time. Calm yourself by closing your eyes and following your breath, in and out, for a count of ten.

2. Focus your attention in the center of your head, in the region near the pineal gland. Sound the *Om* and imagine the golden cable

extending upward as it links your etheric, emotional, and mental bodies with your soul.

3. Formulate your question or problem.

4. Lift your question upward to the soul via the triple cable. Hold your mind still in the light of the soul for as long possible.

5. Imagine the lower mind as the interpreter of information from the soul. Visualize the information you need gently trickling down from the soul to your lower mind and from your lower mind to your brain.

6. Make a note in your journal of any information you receive. Be aware that the information may come in the form of words, pictures, or symbols. Don't worry if you fail to receive an answer to your question. This is a slow process, and success will come by degrees through your persistent and steady effort to build the bridge of communication between the lower mind and your soul.

It is important that you carefully evaluate any information or guidance you receive. In an article on this topic, Corinne McLaughlin writes that true spiritual guidance will include the following elements:

1. It serves the good of the whole.

2. It focuses on helping others and is inclusive, not separative.

3. It inspires and empowers you.

4. It suggests or advises only; it never demands the surrender of your free will.

5. It is in alignment with your personal ethics.

6. It presents new and creative information relevant to the next step in your spiritual evolution.

7. It is received through the head, heart, and throat chakras, or centers, functioning in unison.[19]

Solitude and Silence

Regular periods of silence and solitude are necessary to cultivate a relationship with your soul. If it is at all possible, give yourself time alone every day. Leave your cell phone behind and take a solitary walk, work in your garden, or just sit on your back porch. The Tibetans have a saying, "In solitude the rose of the soul flourishes; in solitude the divine self can speak; in solitude the faculties and the graces of the higher self can take root and blossom in the personality."[20] We need a daily dose of solitude to hear the subtle voice of our souls. As I mentioned in my story about the magazine, it was only when I took a break from my frenetic job search and spent the day working in my garden that I got the information I needed.

Silence deepens the experience of solitude. Mother Teresa considered silence—what she called "the language of God"—to be the most important of all spiritual disciplines. Writing on the virtue of silence, Pope Paul VI has said that "commotion, din . . . and feverish activity . . . all threaten man's inner awareness. If only we could once again appreciate the great value of silence. . . . We need this wonderful state of mind, beset as we are by the cacophony of strident protests and conflicting claims so characteristic of these turbulent times."[21]

In a world where the "din" now includes the 24/7 bombardment of cell-phone calls, text messages, and e-mail, the practice of silence is more important than ever. It is only through silence that we can hear the subtle notes of the higher worlds. The Sufi poet Rumi expresses this beautifully in the following poem:

> There is a way between voice and presence
> where information flows.
> In disciplined silence it opens.
> With wandering talk it closes.[22]

During the founding of the Findhorn community, Eileen Caddy lived in a tiny trailer with five other people—her husband, Peter, their three small children, and their friend and coworker Dorothy Maclean. In the winter, Eileen had only one option for silence and solitude—a public bathroom. As she writes in *The Findhorn Garden*, "I had to learn to put my communion with the God within before anything else. I had to learn to be still. . . . With six of us packed into that tiny [trailer], the only place I could go for complete silence was down to the public toilets. . . . I'd bundle up against the cold and sit there for two or three hours every night. It was [the one] place where I could shut the door and have no interruptions. Ridiculous as it may seem, it was actually quite lovely."[23]

Michal Eastcott also writes on the value of silence: "Silence is no passive thing. It is a vibrant presence that fills any vacuum. . . . The old adage 'silence is golden' means more than just that it is safe or wise. It means that it is 'gold' in the sense of being filled with light. In its secret depths, power is generated, problems are solved, realizations are reached, sensitivity is developed. . . . We are recharged, regenerated and renewed."[24]

The Everyday Genius

When we build our bridge to the soul, we become "receiving stations" for the transmission and distribution of spiritual ideas and wisdom. When we have the ability to bring the treasures of the higher kingdoms down to earth, we join the ranks of those people we call "geniuses." True genius, Bailey writes, "is ever an expression of the soul."[25] Today, our famous artists, writers, scientists, and entrepreneurs are seen as rare and special beings endowed with gifts and talents beyond the normal human functioning. Yet, as many have described, their genius is simply the result of their contact with the subtle worlds. The creative leaps and inspired thinking that have led to their great works of art, discoveries, and inventions came from their connection to the soul.

As I've mentioned, the downflow of soul light has a physical effect on the brain, awakening new and higher brain cells. As more of us get in touch with the light of our souls, these "supernormal" states will be increasingly regarded as a normal and natural part of our human equipment. Genius will no longer be regarded as a rare and random event but an experience that each of us can cultivate.

Imagine the inspired writing, the beautiful works of art, the groundbreaking inventions, and the new healing techniques we will bring to the world as the soul in each of us unfolds. Imagine a critical mass of people working for the greater good, with the goal of making the world a place of peace and joy for the entire human family.

This is the future that awaits us—a future in which we will regularly access and use the wisdom from above in our day-to-day lives. As citizens of both the physical and spiritual worlds, we will stand, in Rumi's words, "at the doorsill where the two worlds touch."[26] As Helena Blavatsky writes in *The Secret Doctrine,*

> The subject of esoteric training may be looked at as the process wherein we learn to live the vertical and horizontal life at the same time. To do this we have to live at the very center where the vertical stream of energy—[coming down from the soul] and the many forces [from our horizontal relationships] meet and cross. This means the establishing of two relationships simultaneously: the relation with the soul . . . which puts us in touch with the soul in all forms, and the relationship with our environment . . . the world, and the entire human family. To do this effectively, we must learn to stand at the center.[27]

Blavatsky also tells us that the sense of responsibility is one of the first indications of soul contact. In the next chapter, I will introduce you to people who, guided by the light of their souls, are living lives of spiritual purpose and service.

Chapter Eight

Become a World Server

I slept and dreamt that life was joy
I awoke and saw that life was service
I acted and behold, service was joy.

—Rabindranath Tagore

When we make contact with the soul, our life purpose—our service to humanity—becomes clear. Each of us has a unique contribution to make to the world; and, at this critical hour, we are all urgently needed.

Today, there are people all over the world who are dedicating their lives to service. According to the Wisdom teachings, those of us with the impulse to serve belong to a group called the "New Group of World Servers."[1] This group has no formal organization, no headquarters, and no outer structure. It includes people in every country and in every field. This group is held together only by an attitude of mind: an international vision of unity, cooperation, and peace. As Alice Bailey writes, "Every man and woman in every country who is working to heal the breaches between people, to evoke the sense of brotherhood, to foster the sense of mutual interrelation, and who see no racial, national or religious barriers, is a member of the New Group of World Servers, even if he or she has never heard of it in those terms."[2]

Motivated by the promptings of their souls, these servers are working to usher in a more peaceful, sustainable, and compassionate world. This group includes humanitarians, educators, politicians, scientists, financers, environmentalists, entrepreneurs, artists, writers, and all men and women of goodwill.

Encoded in your soul is your true life purpose. In this chapter, I will show you how to listen to the subtle voice of your soul to discover the unique contribution you can make to the world. I will also show you how to serve on the inner planes to increase the flow of spiritual energy in the world.

In the past, those with a spiritual calling often locked themselves away in convents or monasteries. The spiritual inspiration and wisdom they received was not used to help others. The blessings of the soul are not ours alone: as the light of the soul pours into our hearts and minds, it is our duty to circulate and share this divine energy with the world. As Pema Chödrön writes in *The Places that Scare You: A Guide to Fearlessness in Difficult Times*, "Few of us are satisfied with retreating from the world and just working on ourselves. We want our training to manifest and be of benefit. The bodhisattva-warrior, therefore, makes a vow to wake up not just for himself but for the welfare of all beings."[3]

SERVICE AND PHILANTHROPY

The awakening soul can be seen in the increased focus on philanthropy in the world today. The word *philanthropy*—from the Greek *philos*, or "loving," and *anthropos*, for "human being" or "humanity"— is defined as the "love for all humanity" or the "desire to benefit humanity." If you turn on the nightly news, you'll see movie stars like

Angelina Jolie, Brad Pitt, and George Clooney using their celebrity to promote a variety of humanitarian causes. You'll hear about Warren Buffet and Bill and Melinda Gates's Giving Pledge, a campaign that invites billionaires in the United States to donate the majority of their wealth to philanthropic causes. To date, ninety-three billionaires have taken the pledge, including Facebook founder Mark Zuckerberg; former New York Mayor Michael Bloomberg; and Star Wars creator, George Lucas. Buffett, who sees the pledge as a way to address society's most pressing problems, also plans to meet with wealthy individuals in India and China with the hope that his idea will spread worldwide.[4]

Service to others is an integral part of every spiritual tradition. Christians are taught that "it is more blessed to give than to receive" (Acts 20:35), and many regularly tithe 10 percent of their income to the church. The Bible tells us that when we freely give to others, the "windows of heaven" are opened and blessings of God are poured down upon us (Mal. 3:10).

In the Jewish tradition, the act of giving to others is called *tzedakah*. This Hebrew word is often translated as "charity" but has its root in the word *tzedek*, or "justice." Giving to those in need is considered to be an act of fairness or righteousness. Tzedakah is traditionally 10 percent of each person's income, and even the poor are expected to give part of what they receive to others. Tzedakah is considered by many to be God's way of allowing human beings to be partners in the divine process of sustaining life. Another Jewish tradition is that of *gemilut hasadim*. This term refers to an act of loving-kindness in which one offers assistance or time to others. It is widely believed that donors benefit from tzedakah as much as or more than their recipients do.[5]

In Buddhism, the practice of giving to others is called *dana-paramita*. *Dana* is a Sanskrit word meaning "generosity" or "giving," while *paramita* means "perfect" or "perfection." *Dana-paramita* refers to the perfection of giving—the act of unconditional generosity to others. This term does not refer only to material giving. The practice of dana-paramita also means giving unconditional love and compassion to others.[6]

Charitable giving is also one of the five pillars of the Islamic faith. The act of giving is called *zakat*, an Arabic word meaning to "purify" and to "grow." Muslims are required to give 2.5 percent of any "extra wealth" that remains after their own basic needs are met. They believe the act of giving to others purifies their soul and increases their own prosperity. Giving additional monies to charity is called *sadaqah*, an Arabic word meaning "truth" and "honesty." Sadaqah can be given at any time and in any amount.[7]

THE SCIENCE OF SERVICE

In the United States alone, there are now over one million charities, and 70 percent of US households donate money each year.[8] We know that giving to others opens our hearts, but there is also evidence that the impulse to give may be hardwired within us. Research shows that the act of giving lights up the pleasure centers in our brains; it is also associated with lower levels of stress hormones, like cortisol, and a reduced risk of depression, illness, and mortality.[9]

Andy Mackie is one example. Mackie was a retired horse trainer who lived in a small camper in a rural section of Washington State. By the late 1990s, he had had a series of heart attacks and at least ten heart surgeries. After his ninth surgery, in their attempt to keep him alive, his doctors had prescribed a total of fifteen different medications. Not only were the medications expensive, they had nasty side effects, too. One day Mackie made a decision: he would throw away the medications and spend his final days pursuing his dream of giving free music lessons to any child who wanted to learn an instrument. He used the money he would have spent at the pharmacy to buy three hundred harmonicas and offered lessons to the kids at a local school. To his doctor's surprise, Mackie didn't die that month—or the next.

For the next twelve years, Mackie continued to give away harmonicas and free music lessons. He also started a foundation that provided free string instruments, lessons, and scholarships to any child who wanted to learn. He taught over twenty thousand children to play the harmonica and more than a thousand to play stringed instruments. Mackie, who finally died in late 2011, believed it was the joy of helping others that kept him alive. "I can't explain the joy," Mackie told one interviewer. "I don't think Bill Gates feels any richer inside than I do."[10]

A Hedge Fund for Humanity

In 1986, Gene Lang, the billionaire philanthropist who created the "I Have a Dream Foundation" to fund college tuition for inner city kids, was interviewed on *60 Minutes*. After watching that interview, Paul Tudor Jones, a wealthy hedge-fund manager, knew that his life had changed forever. Immediately after the program ended, he picked up the phone and called Lang to ask how he could create a similar charitable foundation.

As Jones explained in his own *60 Minutes* interview twenty-seven years later, "There was probably a hole in my soul, and I just didn't know it at the time. This man had suddenly showed me the joy of giving, and I knew then that there was a whole new journey ahead of me."[11]

This journey eventually led to the creation of the Robin Hood Foundation, a New York City charity that solicits money from the wealthy to fund services for New York City's neediest citizens. In the last twenty-five years, this "hedge fund for humanity" has distributed more than 1.25 billion dollars to hundreds of soup kitchens, homeless shelters, schools, and job training programs. Jones and his board members—primarily other hedge fund managers—cover all the administrative costs, so that literally every penny donated goes to help families in need.

Jones and his wife, Sonia, have also recently funded the Contemplative Science Center at the University of Virginia, his alma mater, to explore contemplative practices, values, and ideas. The center's focus on meditation, yoga, and mindfulness training will include ongoing studies of ways in which these disciplines can be incorporated into the university's medical, nursing, and education programs.

Jones, who continues to manage the Tutor Investment Corporation, his thirteen-billion-dollar hedge fund, has told interviewers that he works only so that he can continue to fund his philanthropic ventures: "You cannot have significance in this life if it's all about you. You get your significance, you find your joy in life, through service and sacrifice. It's pure and simple."[12]

For some people it's a crisis or a life-threatening illness that reorients their lives to service. Jan Skogstrom is the founder of Spirit United, an interfaith church in Minneapolis. Spirit United offers educational programs on a wide variety of spiritual traditions and a Sunday service that honors all traditions and faiths.

Skogstrom was a college professor in 1995 when she developed life-threatening complications after gallstone surgery. As she explained to me,

After my surgery, I was in and out of the hospital for four months. When I returned home, I still needed intravenous feeding and the doctors weren't sure I would pull though. I could barely function and spent most of my time in bed just watching the sun move across the floorboards and listening to the birds outside my window.

My husband was also a teacher, and we had built a comfortable life together. I wanted to return to that life, but thinking about the future was just too painful; I knew I might need feeding tubes for the rest of my life. Since I couldn't do much more than just "be," I began to practice living in the present moment and disciplined myself not to think of the past or the future. It was in this period of deep silence that I became more attuned to the guidance of my soul. As I began to recover, my ideas about the future started to shift. I had been ordained as a minister, and I started to think about creating an interfaith church.

I wasn't entirely comfortable with this idea, since my life would change so radically. I would have to leave my wonderful job and the comfortable life my husband and I had built. My husband was not interested in alternative spirituality, and I worried that I could jeopardize my marriage. Still, it felt as though there was a light hand on my back, moving me forward. At that time, there was no interfaith church in Minneapolis, and I was fearful about publicly taking on a minister's role. Even so, I knew that if I didn't do what my soul was calling me to do, my life would no longer feel authentic. It was that feeling of being called that propelled me forward. Starting Spirit United was the most challenging and most rewarding thing I've ever done. In the nine years that I ran Spirit United, I felt I was, in my own small way, contributing to the greater plan of humanity.[13]

Corinne McLaughlin had a similar experience. At midnight on Christmas Eve, 1976, she was meditating in the sanctuary at the Findhorn community in Scotland. Miserable after a string of failed relationships, she asked for guidance. Why did she continue to attract relationships that ended so painfully? Why couldn't she find the right man? Just then, as she explains in her book *The Practical Visionary*, "my soul seemed to whisper to me, 'You didn't come to Earth to find the perfect relationship. You came here to serve humanity in some way.'" As she realized that she needed to release her attachment to finding the perfect mate and focus instead on her higher purpose, she experienced an "inflow of light" that circulated throughout her entire body:

> It felt like a light bulb was turning on in my head each time I took a breath. The light seemed to come from above and below me as it circulated through my body. The next day, I knew that something very powerful had happened, but I wasn't quite sure what it was. My vision had expanded and I realized that my heart felt more open to humanity as a whole. I was more concerned about the suffering in the world. In the days that followed, I began to feel a true sense of inner peace and a clear sense of purpose for the first time in my life. I was happy to become more deeply immersed in my work and service, instead of always looking for a romantic relationship to fulfill me.[14]

McLaughlin met Gordon Davidson, her husband of thirty-four years, three months later. Together they have coauthored several books on the Ageless Wisdom teachings; they also founded the Center for Visionary Leadership to help people develop the inner spiritual resources they need to become effective leaders. They promote the application of spiritual values in all fields, with a special emphasis on business and politics. They offer seminars for the general public, as well as customized trainings, consulting, and coaching to a wide variety of business, government, and nonprofit organizations. Their website offers a variety of easy-to-use spiritual practices and articles from their e-newsletter, *Soul Light*.[15]

Our passions, the things we care most about, are whispers from our souls that can guide us to a particular career or service. I was a kid who loved books and magazines. When I was eight or nine, I read a novel about a girl my age who had her own column in a daily newspaper. The drawing on the cover showed a young girl in a green visor, hunched over a typewriter in a pool of yellow light. The first time I saw that book, something clicked, and I read it over and over. I stared at the cover and knew, without a doubt, that I wanted to be that girl. A few years later, I started a newsletter for my sixth-grade classmates, and I've been involved in publishing, in one form or another, ever since.

Kenneth Bowser has spent the last forty years studying the history and practice of astrology. After his first astrology reading, he developed a passionate interest in the subject that led him to research both the history and astronomical facts related to the subject. Studying the work of scholars who had translated the ancient astronomical and astrological texts, he realized that the original zodiac was based on the stars, rather than the seasons, as it is usually practiced in Europe and the United States. He is now playing a major role in bringing the original practice of astrology back in the West.[16]

Corinne McLaughlin recommends matching our skills and passions with the needs of the world. As she explained to me, "When you bring three things together—your gifts and skills, your own particular passion, and the needs of the world—you find the 'sweet spot,' the area where you can make your greatest contribution."[17] She also points out that there should be a sense of joy in our service. If there isn't, we may not be in the right field or on the right path.

What are you passionate about? Do you have a passionate interest in spirituality, health, politics, business, science, technology, the environment, media, or the arts? How can you use your unique gifts and talents to further the evolutionary goal of cooperation, unity, and peace?

The following meditation has been adapted from the Lucis Trust. If you are not sure how to put your gifts and talents to work, use this meditation to discover the unique contribution you can make to the world.

MEDITATION ON SERVICE

1. Give yourself fifteen minutes of uninterrupted quiet time. Calm yourself by closing your eyes and following your breath, in and out, for a count of ten.

2. When you are ready, use your creative imagination to lift your consciousness to a focal point outside and above your head. See this as the analytical, lower mind, now still and receptive. Project a line of light upward to the soul center, seeing the soul as a brilliant sun, a radiant source of energy. As you link with your soul, silently repeat the following mantra:

> I am the soul,
> I am the light divine.
> I am love, I am will,
> I am fixed design.

3. Take a deep breath and, holding your mind steady in the light, meditate for fifteen minutes on the following question: "How can I serve?"

Listen inwardly for the subtle voice of your soul. At the end of the meditation period, allow any thoughts or images you receive to trickle down gently from the soul to your lower mind, and from the lower mind to your brain.

Take a moment to collect your thoughts, and when you are ready, end the meditation by silently sounding the *Om*. Visualize a pure white light pouring down from your soul, illuminating your mind, calming your emotions, and invigorating your physical body. Send out this incoming light and love to your fellow servers, your family and friends, and all those in need of healing.

Repeat this prayer or make up your own:

May the light of my soul guide and direct my day.
May I be useful in service to my fellow human beings.
May I receive the assistance I need to do my part in the great work.

When you have finished, write down any information you have received. Be aware that your answer may come in a dream or an intuition that leads you to pick up a book, explore a particular group or organization, research a new field, or reach out to a friend or colleague. Also be on the lookout for subtle nudges from your soul that might lead you in an unexpected direction.

Barbara Valocore was a singer with the Los Angeles Opera when her father, Paul Hancock, sold the cable television business he had created in Connecticut to a large media company. He and his wife and daughter decided to use the five-million-dollar profit to create a charitable foundation. Valocore, a long-time student of the Ageless Wisdom, knew she wanted to use the money to benefit humanity in some way.

In 1992, she established the Lifebridge Foundation to support organizations and individuals with cultural, educational, or scientific projects that would promote the concept of the oneness of humanity and the interconnectedness of all life.

Between 1993 and 2005, the Lifebridge Foundation provided funding for hundreds of groups and individuals whose projects reflected the oneness perspective. These diverse projects included Bridges to Community, a nonprofit group that takes volunteers to developing countries to work on construction, health, and environmental projects; World Citizen Diplomats, a group that sponsors "peace caravans" of ordinary citizens who travel the world to promote international and intercultural understanding; and the Prayer Vigil for the Earth, an annual event in which people of diverse faiths, cultures, and ethnic backgrounds gather on the Mall in Washington, DC, to pray for harmony among all people and the planet.

Barbara first got the idea to create Lifebridge Sanctuary, a retreat center where social visionaries could nurture their inspiration and creative ideas, in 1995:

> Every time I drove by a real estate "for sale" sign, something nudged me. . . . I wasn't sure what to make of it at first, but one day as I was driving near my home in upstate New York, I saw a property for sale with a view of the Catskill Mountains and something happened to me. I thought, "There is something I'm supposed to do here." I called a realtor and asked to look at the property.

As I looked at the panoramic view of the mountains, I thought about how great it would be to create a retreat on this beautiful property.

The impression came during my morning meditation. I was asked to create the sanctuary, but I knew I needed more guidance—I was a singer, not a builder. As I continued to meditate, I kept my mind open, listened deeply, and one day, the design of the building just popped into my head.[18]

The sanctuary, which opened in 2005, is a twelve-thousand-square-foot, hand-crafted green facility on ninety-five acres in New York's Hudson Valley, just eighty-five miles north of New York City. The meeting spaces hold up to sixty people during the day and thirty-six overnight. The sanctuary hosts groups focused on nonviolent communication, Qigong, and other related subjects.

"The building is part of the charitable purpose of Lifebridge Foundation, and we accept groups that are aligned with our mission," she told me. "We are able to underwrite some of the costs, which makes the price affordable for nonprofits. Our goal is to support these groups as they do their own service work in the world."[19]

Strengthen Your Connection to the New Group of World Servers

If you are reading this book, you are likely to be a member of the New Group of World Servers. To strengthen your connection to this group, take a moment to say the following prayer every afternoon at 5:00 pm. It can be done anywhere and takes just a few seconds.

May the power of the One Life pour through the group of all true servers.

May the love of the One Soul characterize the lives of all who seek to aid the Great Ones.

May I fulfill my part in the One Work through self-forgetfulness, harmlessness and right speech.

There are also a number of ways that we can serve on the inner planes to increase the flow of divine energy in the world. The only qualifications for this type of planetary service are an open heart and a desire to help humanity during this critical period.

I've included four service-oriented meditations below. Choose the ones that feel right to you. These meditations were also adapted from the Lucis Trust.

Attract Money for Spiritual Purposes

In 2013, the defense budget of the Unites States was almost seven hundred billion dollars. Worldwide, billions more are spent every year on the development and production of new weapons. What if even a fraction of that money were spent on furthering the spiritual welfare of humanity?

This meditation can be used to direct money to spiritual groups, causes, and individuals and to increase the flow of money for your own service projects. Do this meditation every Sunday morning. Put aside a sum of money each week to donate to a specific group or individual—it doesn't matter if it is large or small. Remember that "to those who give, it shall be given so that they can give again."[20]

Visualize money as a stream of flowing, golden energy, and say the following invocative prayer:

> I ask that vast sums of money be made available to the New Group of World Servers. Let the hearts of men everywhere be touched so that they may give to the work of all true servers.

Visualize the work done by a specific group or individual you want to support. See unlimited sums of money pouring into their hands. Visualize their work expanding, and think about the good this money will do.

Visualize money pouring into your own service projects, and think about the good you will do for the world with your increased resources. Then say aloud:

> I ask for the needed money for _____.

Once per month, mail your check to the group or individual you have chosen to support.

Join a Triangle Network

The Triangle Network is another type of world service. Members of this network use creative thought to circulate spiritual energies throughout the world.

A triangle is created by three people who link, each day, for a few minutes of creative meditation. Each member invokes the energies of unity and goodwill and visualizes these energies circulating throughout the three points of the triangle before flowing down to the earth.

The triangle, symbolic of the spiritual trinity in all religions, is the basic energy pattern within the universe. The daily work of thousands of people around the world has created a network of triangles that surround the planet. The focused intent of each triangle member creates a channel for the downpouring of spiritual light and love.

This service takes only a few minutes per day and can be done by anyone, anywhere in the world. It's not necessary for triangle members to live in the same location or to synchronize the timing of each meditation. Once the triangle has been built and vitalized, it can be brought to life by any of the three members. If you would like to participate, invite two friends to help you create your triangle. If you need help finding triangle partners, turn to the resources page in the back of this book.

Follow these steps:

1. Give yourself five minutes of quiet, uninterrupted time. Using your creative imagination, link mentally with the other two members of your triangle. Visualize your triangle as an essential part of the worldwide triangles network.

2. Visualize love and light flowing into each of the three points of your triangle, circulating around the triangle from point to point and flowing out through the network of triangles that surround the planet and into the hearts and minds of all men and women.

3. Sound the Great Invocation (see page 118) silently or aloud. As you repeat each stanza, visualize the network acting as a link between the spiritual hierarchy and humanity, and each triangle member as a channel through which light, love, and divine purpose flow into the world. If it feels right, also take a moment to

imagine an abundance of spiritual energy flowing out to a particular country—one at war or suffering from a natural disaster—or a particular person in need.

Join a Full-Moon Meditation Group

Another way to increase the flow of spiritual energy in the world is to join or start a full-moon meditation group. The full-moon period provides a unique opportunity work more closely with the spiritual beings who guide our planet. The unimpeded alignment between the sun and the earth makes it easier to access energy from the higher worlds.

The group formation creates a channel for both the vertical and horizontal distribution of divine energy. As we distribute this energy to the hearts and minds of all people, we strengthen the link between the human and spiritual kingdoms.

The spiritual energies available for distribution during each full-moon period are related to the zodiac sign of that month. For a list of groups, or instructions on how to start a group, turn to the resources page in this book.

Full-Moon Meditation: Letting in the Light

Leader: We affirm our membership within the New Group of World Servers, mediating between the Hierarchy and humanity.

Group: I am one with my group brothers and sisters, and all that I have is theirs:
May the love that is in my soul pour forth to them.
May the strength that is in me lift and aid them.
May the thoughts that my soul creates reach and encourage them.

Now each participant turns inward for the following meditation:

1. Calm yourself by closing your eyes and following your breath, in and out, for a count of ten.

2. Project a line of lighted energy toward the spiritual Hierarchy of the planet, and open yourself to the extraplanetary energies now available.

3. Focused within the light of the Hierarchy, hold the contemplative mind open to the light and love seeking to externalize on Earth.

4. Reflect on the monthly seed thought, using the zodiacal sign appropriate for each month as follows:

Aries:	I come forth and from the plane of mind, I rule.
Taurus:	I see, and when the eye is opened, all is light.
Gemini:	I recognize my other self, and in the waning of that self, I grow.
Cancer:	I build a lighted house and dwell within.
Virgo:	I am the mother and the child. I am God; I am matter.
Libra:	I choose the way that leads between the two great lines of force.
Scorpio:	I am the warrior, and I emerge triumphant from the battle.
Sagittarius:	I see the goal. I reach that goal and then see another.
Capricorn:	I am lost in the light supernal, yet on that light I turn my back.
Aquarius:	Water of life am I, poured forth for thirsty men.
Pisces:	I leave the Father's home, and turning back, I save.

5. Using your creative imagination, visualize the energies of light, love, and the goodwill pouring down from the Hierarchy to the Group of World Servers and out to the entire planet.

6. End your meditation, open your eyes, and rejoin the group. Together, sound the affirmation:

> Group: In the center of all Love I stand.
> From that center I, the soul, will move outward.
> From that center I, the one who serves, will work.
> May the love of the divine Self be shed abroad, in my heart, through my group, and throughout the world.

As you sound the Great Invocation, visualize the outpouring of light and love from the spiritual Hierarchy touching the hearts and minds of all humanity.

Join the World-Goodwill Meditation Group

World Goodwill is a nongovernmental organization accredited with the United Nation's Department of Public Information. This movement was established to encourage spiritual solutions to the problems of the world. Founded on the principles of brotherhood, human unity, sharing, and cooperation, it provides education and assistance to individuals and groups.

In addition to its educational activities, the organization has formed a weekly goodwill meditation group to increase the flow of goodwill in the world. This worldwide group is open to anyone who wants to participate in this planetary service. Goodwill is love in action, and the meditation is used to promote a cooperative attitude in world affairs.

In this meditation, you will work at the center of both your horizontal and vertical relationships. Our horizontal relationships extend from our friends and family to the entire community of nations on earth. Our vertical relationships include our contact with the spiritual Hierarchy, God, and the universe. During this meditation, you will function as a channel for the inflowing energy of goodwill from the higher planes. You will then radiate this vital, harmonizing energy throughout your entire horizontal network.

The group members try to synchronize their work by meditating at twelve o'clock noon on Wednesdays—the midpoint of the week. However, the meditation work can be effectively done whenever and as often as you choose.

Meditation on Goodwill: Stage One

1. Link up in thought with the people throughout the world who are working with this meditation group.

2. Reflect on your web of relationships. You are related to:

   - Your family
   - Your community
   - Your nation
   - The world of nations
   - The one humanity made up of all races and nations.

3. Use this prayer of unification:

   > The souls of men are one and I am one with them.
   > I seek to love, not hate;
   > I seek to serve and not exact due service;
   > I seek to heal, not hurt.
   > Let the soul control the outer form and life,
   > And bring to light the love
   > That underlies all the events in our world.

Let vision and insight come.
Let the future stand revealed.
Let inner union demonstrate and outer cleavages be gone.
Let love prevail.
Let all men love.

Meditation on Goodwill: Stage Two

1. Reflect on your own and humanity's relationship with the spiritual Hierarchy—the inner government of the planet.

2. Imagine that you are standing within the center of the spiritual Hierarchy and are immersed in the consciousness of the Christ.

3. As you maintain that high point of contact, let your thoughts reach out to include all members of the human family in whom the energy of goodwill is active.

4. Silently voice the affirmation:

   In the center of all love I stand;
   From that center I, the soul, will move outward;
   From that center I, the one who serves, will work.
   May the love of the divine Self be shed abroad
   In my heart, through my group, and throughout the world.

Meditation on Goodwill: Stage Three

1. Visualize the energy of love flowing from the spiritual Hierarchy, through the men and women of goodwill, and into human hearts and minds, infusing them with goodwill and creating loving and harmonious human relationships.

2. Meditate on ways of spreading goodwill, creating right human relationships, and restoring peace on Earth.

3. Realize that you are helping to build a channel between the spiritual Hierarchy and humanity, through which the energy of goodwill may flow, uniting the human family, solving its problems, and healing all differences and cleavages.

4. Linked in thought with men and women of goodwill all over the world, say the Great Invocation. Say it with deliberation and full commitment to its meaning, knowing that you are radiating its potent energies to humanity:

> From the point of Light within the Mind of God
> Let light stream forth into the minds of men.
> Let Light descend on Earth.
>
> From the point of Love within the Heart of God
> Let love stream forth into the hearts of men.
> May Christ return to Earth.
>
> From the center where the Will of God is known
> Let purpose guide the little wills of men—
> The purpose which the Masters know and serve.
>
> From the center which we call the race of men
> Let the Plan of Love and Light work out
> And may it seal the door where evil dwells.
> Let Light and Love and Power restore the Plan on Earth.

TEACH YOUR CHILDREN WELL

Beyond practicing the above meditations, there is another type of world service that is actually very simple: teach your children to think of themselves as world citizens. Our educational system prepares us to compete: first with other students for the best grades, jobs, status, and money; and later, with other countries for the best weapons, technology, and access to natural resources.

Our history books are largely the story of battles and conquests. Imagine how the world would change if future generations were taught from an early age to view themselves as interconnected members of the human family—with no national, racial, or religious barriers. If the leaders of tomorrow were taught to work for the greater good of all, war would eventually give way to peace, international unity, and cooperation. If our children were taught to respect all faiths and to view service to others as the highest ideal, we could create a new reality on earth.

In Tibetan Buddhism, initiates take a vow to return to earth until all beings become enlightened. The Wisdom teachings also tell us that our desire to serve will continue after our own evolution on earth is complete. This teaching is illustrated in a lovely quote from an ancient esoteric text:

What dost thou see, Oh! liberated one?
 Many who suffer, Master, who weep and cry for help.
What will thou do, Oh! man of peace?
 Return from whence I came.
Whence comest thou, Pilgrim divine?
 From the lowest depths of darkness, thence upwards into the light.
Where goest thou, Oh! Traveller upon the upward way?
 Back to the depths of darkness, away from the light of day.
Wherefore this step, Oh! Son of God?
 To gather those who stumble in the darkness and light their steps upon the path.
What is the term of service, Oh! Saviour of men?
 I know not, save that whilst one suffers I stay behind and serve.[21]

Notes

Introduction

1. Brown, *Lost Symbol*, 130.
2. Smoley, *Forbidden Faith*, 32.
3. Brown, *Lost Symbol*, 409.
4. Bailey, *Education in the New Age*, 64.
5. Mitchell, *Way of the Explorer*, 143.

Chapter One

Epigraph: Ken Wilber, in Russell, *From Science to God*, 120.
1. Hall, *Secret Teachings*, 195; and Guthrie, *Pythagorean Sourcebook*, 21.
2. Blavatsky, in Barborka, *Divine Plan*, 159, 176.
3. Ibid., 158–64.
4. Smoley and Kinney, *Hidden Wisdom*, 91.
5. Levenda, *Stairway to Heaven*, 124–25.
6. Eliade, *Shamanism*, 120–1, 274–75.
7. Meyer, *Ancient Mysteries*, 200, 209.
8. Sams, *Dancing the Dream*, 6–7.
9. Lansdowne, *Revelation of St. John*, 9, 11.
10. See Ecclesiastes 12.6: "Remember Him before the silver cord is broken and the golden bowl is crushed, the pitcher by the well is shattered and the wheel at the cistern is crushed." In esoteric symbolism, the golden bowl is the etheric body, and the silver cord is the consciousness thread anchored in the head, as explained in chapter 2. This verse refers to the death of the body and is frequently referenced in esoteric books. Many such biblical verses have deeper, more esoteric meanings.

11. Chief Seattle, in Powell, *ESP Enigma*, 169.

12. Mitchell, *Way of the Explorer*, 59.

13. Beauregard and O'Leary, *Spiritual Brain*, 293.

14. Houston, *A Mythic Life*, 65.

15. McTaggart, *The Field*, xv–xviii.

16. Dossey, *Recovering the Soul*, 123–39.

17. Powell, *Mental Body*, 1.

18. www.edgarcayce.org/are/spiritualGrowth.aspx?id=2078.

19. Drayer, *Nicholas and Helena Roerich*, xxiii.

20. Bailey. "Service in the New Age," in *The Beacon*, 8–13.

21. Bailey, *Treatise on White Magic*, 538.

22. Cremo and Thompson, *Forbidden Archeology*, xxiii–xxxi.

23. Blavatsky, in Barborka, *Divine Plan*, 331.

24. Cooper, *Ecstatic Kabbalah*, 25.

25. Blavatsky, in Barborka, *Divine Plan*, 331.

26. Bailey, *The Rays and the Initiations*, 561.

27. Blavatsky, in Barborka, *Divine Plan*, 337.

28. Johnson, *Riding the Ox Home*, 9–11.

CHAPTER TWO

Epigraph: Emanuel Swedenborg, www.swedenborg.com/emanuel-swedenborg
/writings/short-excerpts-and-downloads/all-of-heaven-is-in-a-human-form.

1. Hubbard, *Emergence*, 4.

2. Mishlove, "An Egyptian Journey of the Soul," intuition.org/journey.

3. www.bahaistudies.net/asma/kabir_and_the_kabir_panth.pdf.

4. Yatri, *Unknown Man*, 204–15.

5. Lawrence, in ibid., 242.

6. Roerich, *Heart*, paragraph 388.

7. Merton, in Needleman, *Lost Christianity*, 120.

8. Magor, *Significance of the Heart*, 7–8.

9. Budge, *Egyptian Religion*, 136–182. See also Budge, *The Book of the Dead*.

10. www.planetherbs.com/theory/wood-the-liver-and-gall-bladder.html.

11. weblog.delacour.net/archives/2003/03/telepathy.php.

12. van der Post, *Heart of the Hunter*, 8–9.

13. Roerich, *Hierarchy*, paragraph 106.

14. Buddha's sermon at Rajagaha, www. buddhasutra.com/files/sermon_at _rajagaha.htm.

15. See www.brainyquote.com/quotes/authors/d/dalai_lama.html.

16. de Chardin, in Russell, *From Science to God*, 129.

CHAPTER THREE

Epigraph: Patanjali, in Bailey, *Light of the Soul*, 160–61.

1. Smoley, *Forbidden Faith*, 95.

2. Bailey, *Education in the New Age*, 95.

3. Bailey, *Light of the Soul*, xv.

4. Ibid, 16.

5. Aurobindo, *Future Evolution of Man*, 91.

6. Meyer, ed., *Nag Hammadi Scriptures*, 737–45.

7. Pagels, *Gnostic Gospels*, 132.

8. Meyer, ed., *Nag Hammadi Scriptures*, 30.

9. Ibid., 410–18. *Discourse on the Eighth and Ninth* was the title given to this gospel. The editor writes that the original title was torn off and later "approximately reconstructed." The "Eight and Ninth" refer to the heavenly spheres, the abode of the highest God.

10. Samuel, *Kabbalah Handbook*, 76.

11. Cooper, *Ecstatic Kabbalah*, 3.

12. Izutsu, *Sufism and Taoism*, 18.

13. Rumi, in Shah, *Way of the Sufi*, 249.

14. Ibid., 104.

15. Dyson, *Infinite in All Directions*, 297. Also quoted in Dossey, *Recovering the Soul*, 153.

16. Bohm and Hiley, *Undivided Universe*, 385–86.

17. Dossey, *Recovering the Soul*, 131.

18. Schrödinger, *What Is Life?*, 129.

19. Bohm and Hiley, *Undivided Universe*, 386.

20. See www.gaiamind.com/Teilhard.html.

21. Radin, *Entangled Minds*, 263. See also Hamilton, "Is God All in Your Head?," in *What Is Enlightenment*, 92.

22. Sheldrake, *Sense of Being Stared At*, ix, 279.

23. Krishna, *Wonder of the Brain*, 50.

24. Newberg and Waldman, *How God Changes Your Brain*, 3.

25. Hanson, *Buddha's Brain*, 5.

26. Pearce, *Biology of Transcendence*, 251.

27. Stillman, *Autism and the God Connection*, 6–7. See also http://blog.autismspeaks.org/2010/11/11/what-lies-beneath-brain-connections.

28. Austin, in Davis, "This is Your Brain on Buddha: Dharma and Neuroscience," www.techgnosis.com.

29. Bailey, *Treatise on White Magic*, 59.

30. Krishna, *The Way to Self-Knowledge*, verses 640–51, 94–95, www.kundaliniresearch.org/blog/wp-content/uploads/2011/11/TWTSK.text_.b.pdf.

CHAPTER FOUR

Epigraph: www.quotezine.com/rumi-quotes-25-sayings-change-life.

1. Long, *Secret Science at Work*, 1–71.

2. Keeney, *Ropes to God*, 42.

3. Elkin, *Aboriginal Men of High Degree*, 57. See also Berndt, *A World That Was*, 133, 246.

4. De Mente, *Business Guide to Japan*, 25–27; Matsumoto, *Unspoken Way*, 37.

5. Radin and Schlitz, "Gut Feelings, Intuition, and Emotions," *Journal of Alternative and Complementary Medicine*, 85–91. See also "Go With Your Gut," *What Is Enlightenment?*

6. www.healthypages.com/community/threads/second-brain.19840. See also Gershon, *Second Brain*.

7. Sheldrake, *Sense of Being Stared At*, ix.

8. Ibid., 20, 73.

9. Keeney, *Ropes to God*, 56.

10. Marcia Emery, correspondence with author, May 2010.

11. Sheldrake, *Dogs that Know*, 56–63.

12. See Cranston, *H. P. B.: The Extraordinary Life*, xx, 153–56, 349–60.

13. See Drayer, *Nicholas and Helena Roerich*.

14. Balyoz, *Three Remarkable Women*, 192–93, 211. See also Bailey, *Unfinished Biography*.

15. Thondup, *Hidden Teachings of Tibet*, 61.

16. Radin, *Conscious Universe*, 87.

17. Bailey, *From Intellect to Intuition*, 164.

18. Bailey, *Telepathy and the Etheric Vehicle*, 5. See also Hodgson, *Woodrow Wilson's Right Hand*, epigraph.

19. Sim Simran, interview with the author. See www.simran-singh.com.

20. Abell, *Talks with Great Composers*, 116–17.

21. Ibid., 137–39.

22. Ibid., 86–107.

23. Ibid., 5–7.

24. Ibid.

25. Huttner, *Mystical Delights*, 8.

26. Ibid., 12.

27. www.leonardodavinci.net/quotes.jsp. See also www.britannica
.com/EBchecked/topic/336408/Leonardo-da-Vinci/59786
/Mechanics-and-cosmology.

28. Schuman, "Michelangelo's Hidden Messages," www.michelangelomethod
.com.

29. Kramarik and Foreli, *Akiane*, 7–11, 15, 38. See also Stahura, "Visions of
God," *Pure Inspiration Magazine*, 6–15.

30. De Mente, *Business Guide to Japan*, 32–33.

31. White, *Isaac Newton*, 5, 85. See also Richard Heinberg, "The Hidden
History of Creativity," *Intuition Magazine*, no. 8, 23–24.

32. www.quotes.net/authors/Albert+Einstein.

33. Joan of Arc, *Joan of Arc: In Her Own Words*, 29.

34. Bucke, *Cosmic Consciousness*, 84.

CHAPTER FIVE

Epigraph: www.inspirationboost.com/lao-tzu-quotes.

1. *The Bhagavad Gita*, ch. 6, verses 16–17, in Bailey, *From Intellect to
Intuition*, 78.

2. www.hinduismtoday.com/modules/smartsection/item.php?itemid=5131.

3. Huffines, *Bridge of Light*, 162.

4. D'Adamo and Whitney, *Eat Right 4 Your Type*, 52, 97, 145, 187.

5. Marsha Mason, interview with the author, March 2011.

6. Steven Lumiere, interview with the author, October 2012.

7. Bailey, *Treatise on White Magic*, 84.

8. Huffines, *Bridge of Light*, 162.

9. Cousens, *Spiritual Nutrition*, 246.

10. www.areconnecting.com/eat-local.html#.VAJePGSwJd0.

11. Cousens, *Spiritual Nutrition*, 152.

12. Ibid., 233.

13. Ponticus, in Needleman, *Lost Christianity*, 136–37.

14. www.buddhanet.net/psymed1.htm.

15. Jan Skogstrom, interview with the author, November 2012.

16. Enright's views on compassion in *Forgiveness Is a Choice* appear throughout his book.

17. Dalai Lama, www.dalailama.com/messages/compassion; www.goodreads .com/quotes/search?q=Dalai+Lama+compassion.

18. Steven Lumiere, interview with the author, October 2012.

19. Isherwood and Prabhavananda, *How to Know God*, 144.

20. Bailey, *Treatise on White Magic*, 80.

21. Powell, *Mental Body*, 284.

22. Isherwood and Prabhavananda, *How to Know God*, 176.

23. Eastcott, *Silent Path*, 59.

Chapter Six

Epigraph: www.peacefulday.com/quotes/mind-stillthe-whole-universe -surrenderschuang-tzu.

1. Saraydarian, *Science of Becoming Oneself*, 198.

2. Ibid.,198.

3. Ibid.

4. Keeney, *Ropes to God*, 38–42.

5. Elkin, *Aboriginal Men of High Degree*, 124–26, 142–45.

6. Hall, *Secret Teachings of All Ages*, 271.

7. Saraydarian, *Science of Becoming Oneself*, 198–99.

8. Biema, "Her Agony," *Time* Magazine, 36–43.

9. Michal Eastcott, *Silent Path*, 73–74.

10. Bailey, *From Intellect to Intuition*, 100.

11. Humphreys, *Concentration and Meditation*, 19, 41.

12. Bailey, *From Intellect to Intuition*, 99–100.

13. Isherwood and Prabhavananda, *How to Know God*, 173–75.

14. Bailey, *From Intellect to Intuition*, 133–36.

15. Bailey, *Treatise on White Magic*, 517.

16. Bailey, *From Intellect to Intuition*, 164.

17. Bailey, *Light of the Soul*, 317.

18. Bailey, *From Intellect to Intuition*, 230–31.

19. Lucis Trust, www.lucistrust.org.

20. McLaughlin and Davidson, *Spiritual Politics*, 394.

21. Ibid.

22. The Findhorn Community, *Findhorn Garden*, 36.

23. Steve Nation, interview with the author, March 2014.

24. Steven Lumiere, interview with the author, October 2012.

25. Bailey, *Education in the New Age*, 95.

26. Bailey, *From Intellect to Intuition*, 165.

CHAPTER SEVEN

Epigraph: Emerson, *Selected Essays, Lectures and Poems*, 177.

1. McLaughlin and Davidson, *Spiritual Politics*, 205.

2. White Eagle, *Jesus, Teacher and Healer*, 58.

3. Bailey, *From Bethlehem to Calvary*, 44–45, 99–100, 141, 194, 234–35.

4. Bailey, *Treatise on White Magic*, 60.

5. Pagels, *Beyond Belief*, 231.

6. Pagels, *Gnostic Gospels*, 145.

7. Pagels, *Beyond Belief*, 237.

8. Eastcott, *The Silent Path*.

9. Bauman, *Soul Vision*, 86. More information on Bill Bauman's programs can be found at www. billbauman.net.

10. Ibid., 87.

11. Weintraub, *Silent Night*, 87.

12. Murphy, *Truce*, 81.

13. Ibid., 87.

14. Cherry, *My Enemy, My Friend*, 56, 70.

15. LaUna Huffines, interview with the author, March 2014.

16. Nancy Seifer, interview with the author, April 2014.

17. Martin Vieweg, interview with the author, April 2014.

18. Steve Nation, interview with the author, March 2014.

19. McLaughlin, "Evaluating Spiritual Guidance." The full text of this article can be found at www.visionarylead.org/articles/eval_spiritual _guidance.htm.

20. Bailey, *Treatise on White Magic*, 132.

21. Opus Angelorum, Inc., www.opusangelorum.org/oa_spirituality/six _traits_docs/Silenceandsolitude.html.

22. www.peacefulrivers.homestead.com/Rumipoetry1.html.

23. Caddy, in the Findhorn Community, *The Findhorn Garden*, 37.

24. Eastcott, *Silent Path*, 154.

25. Bailey, *Esoteric Psychology*, 250.

26. www. peacefulrivers.homestead.com/Rumipoetry1.html. From *Essential Rumi* by Coleman Barks.

27. Blavatsky, *Secret Doctrine*, 34.

CHAPTER EIGHT

Epigraph: www.tentmaker.org/Quotes/tagore-quotes.html.

1. See, for instance, Bailey, *Esoteric Psychology*, vol. 2, 636.

2. Ibid., 642–43.

3. Chödrön, *Places that Scare You*, 122.

4. www.givingpledge.org.

5. Clinton, *Giving*, 208. Also see "Judaism 101," www.jewfaq.org /tzedakah.htm.

6. Ibid., 209. See also "The Six Paramitas," www.naljorprisondharmaservice .org/pdf/SixParamitas.htm.

7. Ibid., 208. See also www.islamicity.com/mosque/zakat.

8. Ibid., 13.

9. Nelmark, *Why Good Things Happen*, 2.

10. Steve Hartman, CBS Evening News, New York, May 1, 2009.

11. Ibid., May 5, 2013.

12. www.cbsnews.com/news/modern-day-robin-hood/2.

13. Jan Skogstrom, interview with the author, November, 2012.

14. McLaughlin, *Practical Visionary*, 6.

15. www.visionarylead.org.

16. See www.WesternSiderealAstrology.com.

17. Corinne McLaughlin, interview with the author, April 2014.

18. Barbara Valocore, interview with the author, May 2012.

19. Lifebridge Foundation, www.lifebridge.org.

20. www.lucistrust.org/en/arcane_school/meditation/two_redemptive _meditations.

21. Bailey, *Light of the Soul*, 420.

Works Cited

Abell, Arthur. *Talks with Great Composers*. New York, Philosophical Library, 1955.

Bailey, Alice A. *Education in the New Age*. New York: Lucis Publishing, 1954.

———. *Esoteric Psychology*. 2 vols. New York: Lucis Publishing, 1936–42.

———. *From Bethlehem to Calvary*. New York: Lucis Publishing, 1937.

———. *From Intellect to Intuition*. New York: Lucis Publishing, 1932.

———. *The Light of the Soul: The Yoga Sutras of Patanjali*. New York: Lucis Publishing, 1927.

———. *The Rays and Initiations*. New York: Lucis Publishing, 1960.

———. "Service in the New Age." *The Beacon*, April, 1935. Reprint, Jan/Feb 2006.

———. *Telepathy and the Etheric Vehicle*. New York: Lucis Publishing, 1950.

———. *A Treatise on White Magic*. New York: Lucis Publishing, 1934.

———. *The Unfinished Biography*. New York: Lucis Publishing, 1994.

Balyoz, Harold. *Three Remarkable Women*. 2nd ed. Flagstaff: Altai Publishers, 1986.

Barborka, Geoffrey. *The Divine Plan*. Wheaton, IL: Theosophical Publishing House, 1961.

Bauman, Bill. *Soul Vision: A Modern Mystic Looks at Life through the Eyes of the Soul*. St. George, UT: Center for Soulful Living, 2009.

Beauregard, Mario, and Denyse O'Leary. *The Spiritual Brain: A Neuroscientist's Case for the Existence of the Soul*. San Francisco: HarperOne, 2007.

Berndt, Ronald, and Catherine Berndt. *A World That Was: The Yaraldi of the Murray River and the Lakes, South Australia*. Vancouver: UBC Press, 1993.

Blavatsky, H. P. *The Secret Doctrine: The Synthesis of Science, Religion, and Philosophy*. Originally 2 vols. 1888. Reprint. Edited by Boris de Zirkoff. 3 vols. Wheaton, IL: Quest Books. 1993.

Bohm, David, and B. J. Hiley. *The Undivided Universe: An Ontological Interpretation of Quantum Theory*. Reprint. New York: Routledge, 1995.

Brown, Dan. *The Lost Symbol*. New York: Doubleday, 2009.

Bucke, Richard. *Cosmic Consciousness: A Study in the Evolution of the Human Mind*. Arkana Books, 1991.

Budge, Sir Wallis. *The Book of the Dead: An English Translation of the Chapters and Hymns of the Theban Recension*. New York: Barnes and Noble, 1953.

———. *Egyptian Religion*. Reprint. New York: Bell, 1959.

Cherry, Dan. *My Enemy, My Friend: A Story of Reconciliation from the Vietnam War*. 2nd ed. Bowling Green, KY: Aviation Heritage Park, 2009.

Chödrön, Pema. *The Places that Scare You: A Guide to Fearlessness in Difficult Times*. Boston: Shambhala, 2002.

Clinton, Bill. *Giving: How Each of Us Can Change the World*. New York: Knopf, 2007.

Cooper, David. *Ecstatic Kabbalah*. Boulder: Sounds True, 2005.

Cousens, Gabriel. *Spiritual Nutrition: Six Foundations for Spiritual Life and the Awakening of Kundalini*. Berkeley: North Atlantic, 1986.

Cranston, Sylvia. *H. P. B.: The Extraordinary Life and Influence of Helena Blavatsky, Founder of the Modern Theosophical Movement*. New York: Tarcher/Putnam, 1993.

Cremo, Michael, and Richard Thompson. *Forbidden Archeology: The Hidden History of the Human Race*. Alachua, FL: Govardhan Hill, 1993.

D'Adamo, Peter, and Catherine Whitney. *Eat Right 4 Your Type: The Individualized Diet Solution to Staying Healthy, Living Longer, and Achieving Your Ideal Weight*. New York: Putnam, 1997.

Davis, Erik. "This Is Your Brain on Buddha: Dharma and Neuroscience." www.techgnosis.com.

De Mente, Boye Lafayette. *Business Guide to Japan: A Quick Guide to Opening Doors and Closing Deals*. North Clarendon, VT: Tuttle, 2006.

Dossey, Larry. *Recovering the Soul: A Scientific and Spiritual Search*. New York: Bantam, 1989.

Drayer, Ruth. *Nicholas and Helena Roerich: The Spiritual Journey of Two Great Artists and Peacemakers*. Wheaton, IL: Quest Books, 2005.

Dyson, Freeman. *Infinite in All Directions*. New York: Harper and Row, 1988.

Eastcott, Michal. *The Silent Path: An Introduction to Meditation*. New York: Samuel Weiser, 1969.

Eliade, Mircea. *Shamanism: Archaic Techniques of Ecstasy*. Translated by Willard R. Trask. New York: Bollingen Foundation, 1964.

Elkin, A. P. *Aboriginal Men of High Degree*. New York: St. Martin's Press, 1945.

Emerson, Ralph Waldo. *Selected Essays, Lectures, and Poems*. Reissue edition. New York: Bantam Classics, 1990.

Enright, Robert. *Forgiveness Is a Choice: A Step-by-Step Process for Resolving Anger and Restoring Hope*. Washington, DC: American Psychological Association, 2001.

The Findhorn Community. *The Findhorn Garden*. Forres, SCT: Findhorn Press, 1975.

Gershon, Michael. *The Second Brain: A Groundbreaking New Understanding of Nervous Disorders of the Stomach and Intestine*. New York: Harper Perennial, 1999.

Ghose, Aurobindo. *The Future Evolution of Man: The Divine Life upon Earth*. Twin Lakes, WI: Lotus Press, 2003.

"Go With Your Gut." *What Is Enlightenment?*, no. 25 (May 2004).

Guthrie, Kenneth Sylvan, comp. and trans. *The Pythagorean Sourcebook and Library*. Grand Rapids, MI: PhanesPress, 1987.

Hall, Manly P. *The Secret Teachings of All Ages*. New York: Tarcher/Penguin, Reader's Edition, 2003.

Hamilton, Craig. "Is God All in Your Head?" *What is Enlightenment?* June 2005.

Hanson, Rick. *Buddha's Brain: The Practical Neuroscience of Happiness, Love, and Wisdom*. Oakland: New Harbinger Publications, 2009.

Heinberg, Richard. "The Hidden History of Creativity." *Intuition Magazine*, no. 8 (1995).

Hodgson, Godfrey. *Woodrow Wilson's Right Hand: The Life of Colonel Edward M. House*. Reprint. New Haven, CT: Yale University Press, 2008.

Houston, Jean. *A Mythic Life: Learning to Live Our Greater Story*. San Francisco: HarperSanFrancisco, 1996.

Hubbard, Barbara Marx. *Emergence: The Shift from Ego to Essence.* Charlottesville, VA: Hampton Roads, 2001.

Huffines, LaUna. *Bridge of Light: Tools of Light for Spiritual Transformation.* Tiburon, CA: H. J. Kramer, 1993.

Humphreys, Christmas. *Concentration and Meditation.* London: Buddhist Society, 1935.

Huttner, Hilary. *Mystical Delights.* Incline Village, NV: Frontline, 1996.

Isherwood, Christopher, and Swami Prabhavananda. *How to Know God: The Yoga Aphorisms of Patanjali.* Hollywood: Vedanta Society of Southern California, 1953.

Izutsu, Toshihiko. *Sufism and Taoism: A Comparative Study of Key Philosophical Concepts.* Berkeley: University of California Press, 1984.

Joan of Arc. *Joan of Arc: In Her Own Words.* Translated by Willard R. Trask. New York: Turtle Point Press, 2004.

Johnson, Willard. *Riding the Ox Home: A History of Meditation from Shamanism to Science.* Boston: Beacon Press, 1986.

Keeney, Bradford, ed. *Ropes to God: Experiencing the Bushman Spiritual Universe.* Philadelphia: Ringing Rocks Press, 2003.

Kramarik, Akiane, and Foreli Kramarik. *Akiane: Her Life, Her Art, Her Poetry.* New York: Thomas Nelson, 2006.

Krishna, Gopi. *The Way to Self-Knowledge.* Markdale, Ontario: Institute for Consciousness Research, 1984.

———. *The Wonder of the Brain,* Markdale, Ontario: Institute for Consciousness Research, 1987.

Landsdowne, Zachary. *The Revelation of Saint John: The Path to Soul Initiation.* San Francisco: Weiser, 2006.

Levenda, Peter. *Stairway to Heaven: Chinese Alchemists, Jewish Kabbalists, and the Art of Spiritual Transformation.* New York: Continuum, 2008.

Long, Max Freedom. *The Secret Science at Work: The Huna Method as a Way of Life.* Camarillo, CA: DeVorss, 1953.

Magor, Nancy. *The Significance of the Heart.* Kent, UK: Sundial House, 1972.

Matsumoto, Michihiro. *The Unspoken Way, Haragei: Silence in Japanese Business and Society.* Tokyo: Kodansha, 1988.

McLaughlin, Corinne, *The Practical Visionary: A New World Guide to Spiritual Growth and Social Change*. Unity Village, MO: Unity Books, 2010.

McLaughlin, Corinne, and Gordon Davidson. *Spiritual Politics: Changing the World from the Inside Out*. New York: Ballantine, 1994.

McTaggart, Lynne. *The Field: The Quest for the Secret Force of the Universe*. New York: Harper Collins, 2002.

Meyer, Marvin, ed. *The Ancient Mysteries: A Sourcebook of Sacred Texts of the Mystery Religions of the Ancient Mediterranean World*. New York: Harper and Row, 1987.

———, ed. *The Nag Hammadi Scriptures*. San Francisco: HarperOne, 2007.

Mitchell, Edgar. *The Way of the Explorer: An Apollo Astronaut's Journey through the Material and Mystical Worlds*. New York: G. P. Putnam's Sons, 1996.

Murphy, Jim. *Truce: The Day the Soldiers Stopped Fighting*. New York: Scholastic Press, 2009.

Needleman, Jacob. *Lost Christianity: A Journey of Rediscovery*. New York: Tarcher/Putnam, 2003.

Newberg, Andrew, and Mark Robert Waldman. *How God Changes Your Brain: Breakthrough Findings from a Leading Neuroscientist*. New York: Ballantine, 2009.

Pagels, Elaine. *The Gnostic Gospels*. New York: Vintage, 1979.

———. *Beyond Belief: The Secret Gospel of Thomas*. New York: Vintage, 2004.

Pearce, Joseph Chilton. *The Biology of Transcendence: A Blueprint of the Human Spirit*. Rochester, VT: Park Street Press, 2004.

Post, Stephen, and Jill Neimark. *Why Good Things Happen To Good People: The Exciting New Research that Proves the Link between Doing Good and Living a Longer, Healthier, Happier Life*. New York: Broadway Books, 2007.

Powell, A. E., *The Mental Body*. 3rd ed. Wheaton: IL, Theosophical Publishing House, 1967.

Powell, Diane Hennacy. *The ESP Enigma: The Scientific Case for Psychic Phenomena*. New York: Walker and Company, 2008.

Radin, Dean. *The Conscious Universe: The Scientific Truth of Psychic Phenomena*. San Francisco: HarperSanFrancisco, 1997.

———. *Entangled Minds: Extrasensory Experiences in a Quantum Reality.* New York: Paraview Pocket Books, 2006.

Radin, Dean, and Marilyn J. Schlitz. "Gut Feelings, Intuition, and Emotions: An Exploratory Study." *Journal of Alternative and Complementary Medicine* 11, no. 1 (2005).

Roerich, Helena. *Heart.* New York: Agni Yoga Society, 1932.

———. *Hierarchy.* New York: Agni Yoga Society, 1931.

Russell, Peter. *From Science to God: The Mystery of Consciousness and the Meaning of Light.* Las Vegas: Elf Rock Productions, 2002.

Sams, Jamie. *Dancing the Dream: The Seven Sacred Paths of Human Transformation.* San Francisco: HarperOne, 1999.

Samuel, Gabriella. *The Kabbahah Handbook: A Concise Encyclopedia of Terms and Concepts in Jewish Mysticism.* New York: Tarcher/Penguin, 2007.

Saraydarian, Torkom. *The Science of Becoming Oneself.* Houston: Saraydarian Institute, 1969.

Schrödinger, Erwin. *What Is Life?: With Mind and Matter and Autobiographical Sketches.* Reprint. New York: Cambridge University Press, 2012.

Shah, Idries. *The Way of the Sufi.* London: Octagon, 1968.

Sheldrake, Rupert. *Dogs that Know When Their Owners Are Coming Home and Other Unexplained Powers of Animals.* New York: Crown Books, 1999.

———. *The Sense of Being Stared At and Other Aspects of the Extended Mind.* New York: Crown Books, 2003.

Smoley, Richard. *Forbidden Faith: The Secret History of Gnosticism.* San Francisco: HarperSanFrancisco, 2006.

Smoley, Richard, and Jay Kinney. *Hidden Wisdom: A Guide to the Western Inner Traditions.* New York: Penguin/Putnam, 1999.

Stahura, Barbara. "Visions of God: The Art of Akiane." *Pure Inspiration Magazine,* Winter 2008.

Stillman, William. *Autism and the God Connection.* Naperville, IL: Sourcebooks, 2006.

Thondup, Tulku. *Hidden Teachings of Tibet*. Somerville, MA: Wisdom Publications, 1986.

Van Biema, David. "Her Agony." *Time* Magazine, September 3, 2007.

van der Post, Laurens. *The Heart of the Hunter*. New York: William Morrow, 1961.

Weintraub, Stanley. *Silent Night: The Story of the World War I Christmas Truce*. Reprint. New York: Plume, 2002.

White Eagle. *Jesus, Teacher and Healer*. Camarillo, CA: DeVorss, 2008.

White, Michael. *Isaac Newton: The Last Sorcerer*. New York: Basic Books, 1999.

Yatri. *Unknown Man: The Mysterious Birth of a New Species*. New York: Fireside, 1988.

ADDITIONAL READING

Arrowsmith, Brian. "The Science of the Antahkarana." *The Beacon* (July/August 2005): 20–23.

Austin, James. *Zen and the Brain: Toward an Understanding of Meditation and Consciousness.* Cambridge: MIT Press, 1998.

Bailey, Alice. *Letters on Occult Meditation.* New York: Lucis Publishing, 1922.

Banks, Natalie. *The Golden Thread.* New York: Lucis Publishing, 1963.

Beauregard, Mario. *Brain Wars.* SanFrancisco: HarperOne, 2013.

Begley, Sharon. *Train Your Mind, Change Your Brain: How a New Science Reveals Our Extraordinary Potential to Transform Ourselves.* New York: Ballantine, 2007.

Childre, Doc, and Howard Martin. *The HeartMath Solution.* San Francisco: Harper San Francisco, 1999.

Crawford, Ina. *A Guide to the Mysteries.* London: Lucis Press, 1990.

Dalai Lama. *An Open Heart: Practicing Compassion in Everyday Life.* New York: Little, Brown, 2001.

Dossey, Larry. *One Mind: How Our Individual Mind Is Part of a Greater Consciousness and Why It Matters.* Carlsbad, CA: Hay House, 2013.

Godwin, Gale. *Heart: A Personal Journey through Its Myths and Meanings.* New York: William Morrow, 2001.

Godwin, Joscelyn. *The Golden Thread: The Ageless Wisdom of the Western Mystery Traditions.* Wheaton, IL: Quest Books, 2007.

Goleman, Daniel. *The Meditative Mind: The Varieties of Meditative Experience.* New York: Jeremy Tarcher, 1988.

Gyatso, Kelsang. *Understanding the Mind: The Nature and Power of the Mind.* Glen Spey, NY: Tharpa Publications, 1993.

Harman, Willis. *Higher Creativity: Liberating the Unconscious for Breakthrough Insights.* New York: Jeremy Tarcher, 1984.

Jastrow, Robert. *The Enchanted Loom: Mind in the Universe.* New York: Simon and Schuster, 1981.

Landsdowne, Zachary. *The Chakras and Esoteric Healing.* York Beach, ME: Samuel Weiser, 1986.

Laszlo, Ervin. *Science and the Akashic Field: An Integral Theory of Everything.* Rochester, VT: Inner Traditions, 2004.

Lawlor, Robert. *Voices of the First Day: Awakening in the Aboriginal Dreamtime.* Rochester, VT: Inner Traditions, 1991.

Lipton, Bruce, and Steve Bhaerman. *Spontaneous Evolution: Our Positive Future and a Way to Get There from Here.* Carlsbad, CA: Hay House, 2009.

Marion, Jim. *Putting on the Mind of Christ: The Inner Work of Christian Spirituality.* Charlottesville, VA: Hampton Roads, 2000.

Murphy, Michael, James Redfield, and Sylvia Timbers. *God and the Evolving Universe: The Next Step in Personal Evolution.* New York: Tarcher/Putnam, 2002.

Nash, John. *Quest for the Soul: The Age-Old Search for Our Inner Spiritual Nature.* Bloomington, IN: 1st Books, 2004.

Parrish-Harra, Carol. *Adventures in Meditation.* 3 vols. Tahlequah, OK: Sparrow Hawk Press, 1995–97.

Powell, A. E. *The Astral Body.* Reprint. Wheaton, IL: Theosophical Publishing House, 1927.

———. *The Causal Body.* 3rd ed. Wheaton, IL: Theosophical Publishing House, 1972.

Radin, Dean. *SuperNormal: Science, Yoga, and the Evidence for Extraordinary Psychic Abilities.* New York: Deepak Chopra, 2013.

Russell, Peter. *The Global Brain Awakens: Our Next Evolutionary Leap.* Boston: Element Books, 2000.

Seifer, Nancy, and Martin Vieweg, *When the Soul Awakens: The Path to Spiritual Evolution and a New World Era.* Reston, VA: Gathering Wave Press, 2009.

Sinclair, Sir John. *The Mystical Ladder*. London: Spiritualist Association of Great Britain, 1968.

Smoley, Richard. *Inner Christianity: A Guide to the Esoteric Tradition*. Boston: Shambhala, 2002.

Targ, Russell, and Jane Katra. *Miracles of Mind*. Novato, CA: New World Library, 1998.

Two Disciples. *The Rainbow Bridge*. 4th ed. Danville, CA: The Triune Foundation, 1994.

White Eagle. *The Light Bringer: The Ray of John and Age of Intuition*. Hampshire: White Eagle Publishing Trust, 2001.

Wolf, Fred Alan. *The Spiritual Universe: How Quantum Physics Proves the Existence of the Soul*. New York: Simon and Schuster, 1996.

Zetter, Kim. *Simple Kabbalah: A Guide to the Ancient Mystical Practice and Beliefs*. San Francisco: Weiser, 2007.

Resource Guide

Esoteric Training

The Arcane School
www.lucistrust.org

The School for Esoteric Studies
www.esotericstudies.net

Meditation Mount
www.meditationmount.org

The University of the Seven Rays
www.sevenray.net

Ageless Wisdom Websites

Lucis Trust
www.lucistrust.org

Center for Visionary Leadership
www.visionarylead.org

When the Soul Awakens
www.whenthesoulawakens.org

Path of Light
www.pathoflight.com

Spiritual Healing

Steven Lumiere
www.energyreality.com

John Jones
www.karmiccommunications.com

MEDITATION RESOURCES

www.meditation.com

Full Moon Meditations
www.worldservicegroup.com

The Triangles Network
www.pathoflight.com/content/triangles-network-world-service

World Goodwill
www.lucistrust.org

EDUCATION

The Wisdom School
www.wisdomuniversity.org

TSG Foundation
www.tsgfoundation.org

The Nine Gates Mystery School
www.ninegates.org

RESEARCH

The Institute of Noetic Sciences
www.noetic.org

INDEX

"Throughout history, we humans have thought about our planet and its place and our place in the larger scheme of things. Of course, it has taken modern developments like large telescopes and space craft to begin to assess the true vastness of the universe (or universes) and to realize that our planet is truly like a grain of sand on a very large beach. The galaxies and star systems currently visible with modern technology number in the billions and seem to stretch without end in all directions.

The development of science in the Western world following the great thinking and innovations of Rene Descartes, Johan Kepler and Isaac Newton in the sixteenth and seventeenth centuries allowed science to arise as we now understand it. However, one of Descartes's major tenets—that physicality and spirituality belong to different realms of reality—led to science avoiding the study of consciousness for four hundred years until the twentieth century because it was considered a subject only for religion and philosophy.

The discoveries of Max Planck, Albert Einstein, and other greats of the late nineteenth and early twentieth centuries resulted in the careful studies of the interactions of newly observed subatomic particles. As a result, quantum entanglement, with its property of nonlocality and the mathematics of quantum interactions, is considered the first scientific link in the chain of awareness that leads to understanding consciousness. This early knowledge of the quantum world was in place by the 1920s. However, it has required most of the twentieth century and well into our twenty-first century for science to go beyond "matter and energy" as the basic properties of our observable universe. Consciousness-science is now accepting that "awareness"— the basic property in nature leading to "consciousness"—is a third fundamental property of all existence. To be blunt: our knowledge of nature is not as complete as most contemporary Westerners would like to believe.

However, the great thinkers in the Eastern traditions—beginning notably with Buddhism in India and then spreading to most civilizations of the near and far East during the last five hundred years BC—focused more locally on human mental capabilities. They are the ones who developed the mental disciplines leading to the techniques of thinking, healing, and study that have only become practiced in Western civilizations in recent times. It is always a pleasure for me to welcome new work like Colleen Mauro's *Spiritual Telepathy*, which adds to the growing literature assisting human betterment."

—**Edgar Mitchell**, Apollo 14 Lunar Module Pilot

Quest Books

encourages open-minded inquiry into
world religions, philosophy, science, and the arts
in order to understand the wisdom of the ages,
respect the unity of all life, and help people explore
individual spiritual self-transformation.

Its publications are generously supported by
The Kern Foundation,
a trust committed to Theosophical education.

Quest Books is the imprint of
the Theosophical Publishing House,
a division of the Theosophical Society in America.
For information about programs, literature,
on-line study, membership benefits, and international centers,
see www.theosophical.org
or call 800-669-1571 or (outside the U.S.) 630-668-1571.

Related Quest Titles

*Isis Unveiled: Secrets of the Ancient Wisdom Tradition,
Madame Blavatsky's First Work,* edited by Michael Gomes

The Meditative Path, by John Cianciosi

The Pilgrim Soul: A Path to the Sacred, by Ravi Ravindra

*The Secret Gateway: Modern Theosophy and the
Ancient Wisdom Tradition,* by Edward Abdill

The Transcendent Unity of Religions, by Frithjof Schuon

*The Visionary Window: A Quantum Physicist's
Guide to Enlightenment,* by Amit Goswami

To order books or a complete Quest catalog,
call 800-669-9425 or (outside the U.S.) 630-665-0130.